Cruising
New Zealand Waters

Cruising
New Zealand Waters

A Guide to Shore Facilities

Jane and Michael Burroughs

HR

Published by Heinemann Reed, a division of Octopus Publishing Group
(N.Z.) Ltd, 39 Rawene Road, Birkenhead, Auckland. Associated companies,
branches and representatives throughout the world.

ISBN 0 7900 0062 8

© Jane and Michael Burroughs
First Published 1989

Designed by Graeme Leather
Typeset by Glenfield Graphics, Auckland
Printed by Kim Hup Lee Printing Co. Pte Ltd, Singapore

Contents

The Marlborough – Nelson area

Acknowledgements

We would like to thank the following people for their assistance in the preparation of this book: the staff of the Bay of Islands Maritime and Historic Park, the Hauraki Gulf Maritime Park, the Marlborough Sounds Maritime Park, Abel Tasman National Park, the Marlborough Harbour Board, the Nelson Harbour Board, and the Northland Harbour Board; the Auckland Harbour Board and the Auckland Regional Authority Parks Department; the Department of Conservation, Nelson; Darryl Wilson of Abel Tasman National Park Enterprises; Brian Pollock of Nelson; Tom King Turner and his wife of Nelson; Millie Pickering of Charter Link Marlborough; Russell McClue of Charter Link Auckland; Sue Weston, J. Gardiner, and Gordon and Nancy McLarty, for their photographs; the secretaries of the boating clubs mentioned in this book; Lin and Larry Pardey of Kawau for suggesting we write the book and Mike Bradstock of Auckland for his encouragement in getting it started.

A special acknowledgement to the crew of *Windora*, our cruising companions during much of the research for this book.

Introduction

There are several cruising guides to the waters of New Zealand already found on the bookshelves of boaties. We ourselves are regular users of the Royal Akarana Yacht Club's *Coastal Cruising Handbook* and *Pickmere's Atlas*, for example. So what need for another one?

When we go boating we want to know more than just navigational details. On a day trip, we might want to know whether the beach is suitable for a barbecue; whether there is shade from the sun; what there is for children to do. On a summer cruise, we need to know where to find fresh water, fuel, food supplies and other essentials.

Through this book we want to share knowledge we have gained cruising around New Zealand, in the hope that it will make boating easier for others.

Wherever possible we have used personal experience, but we have also talked to people familiar with particular areas. We have not covered navigation into an anchorage. An up-to-date chart is required for this. However, useful specifics that we particularly noted have been mentioned.

There are many excellent cruising areas in New Zealand. We have not been able to cover them all in this book, but have picked out a few of the more popular and our own particular favourites.

During our travels we have often met overseas sailors and been asked for information which may be common knowledge among locals. We have been pleased to help and have kept them in mind during the writing of this book. For this reason the book includes some information which may be familiar or even obvious to many locals.

Where descriptions use 'left' and 'right' the perspective is from the sea, facing the land. Metric measurements are used, apart from distance over the water, which is measured in nautical miles.

The maps in this book are sketches only to show location of facilities. They are not to scale and should not be used for navigation purposes.

All information in this book has been checked and was correct at the time of writing, but the authors and publisher accept no responsibility for any errors or omissions.

We hope you all enjoy your boating, wherever your home port is.

The Bay of Islands

The Bay of Islands is a beautiful cruising area and people come from all over the world to see it. For many years we regarded it as just a place for tourists. Eventually we visited it in our own boat, discovered its attraction and it is now our home.

Whichever way the wind is blowing there is always a sheltered bay. We rode out Cyclone Bola in March 1988 in one of the Bay's many anchorages. All the essentials such as water, fuel, stores and facilities are available and there are recreational activities for all ages.

Charter boats leave from Russell or Opua where they can stock up on supplies. Boats coming from Auckland arrive in the Bay after rounding Cape Brett. There are several launching ramps for trailer boats depending on where you plan to go for the day.

Camping is allowed on designated parts of Urupukapuka Island so people with runabouts or day sailers can make their base there and spend a few days exploring the area. Alternatively, there are campsites at Paihia, Russell, Jacks Bay and Rawhiti on the mainland.

The Bay of Islands is steeped in history. Russell, once called Kororareka, was New Zealand's first capital. It also had another name – 'the hell-hole of the South Pacific' – in the early nineteenth century when it was a base for whaling ships and their crews.

Today it is a peaceful place, full of character. It does not take long to stroll around the town and on the way you can see New Zealand's oldest church, New Zealand's most picturesque police station and the Bay of Islands Maritime and Historic Park headquarters, amongst other attractions.

A regular ferry service connects Russell with Paihia. Paihia is a modern tourist town and because it is on one of the main routes north it is busier than Russell. There are shops of every description including banks and a post office.

Opua, just off the highway before Paihia, is at the junction of two rivers and is a popular haven for overseas boats visiting New Zealand during the Pacific cyclone season (from November/December to April). The car ferry to Russell runs from here and provides an alternative route to the picturesque but winding back road to Russell.

There are several boat yards in Opua so it is a good place for anyone wishing to make repairs.

The other major town in the Bay of Islands is Kerikeri. Russell, Opua and Paihia are all readily accessible from the open sea and within a short distance of each other, but Kerikeri stands alone at the head of the river and can be reached only at certain stages of the tide. However, it is well worth a visit. Boats making the river trip end up in the Stone Store Basin in front of Kemp House, a mission house built in 1822, and the old stone mission store, which is still trading today.

The township itself is about a kilometre and a half

up the hill to the left of the Stone Store and has all facilities such as shops, banks, post office, doctor and garages. There are also many lovely walks around Kerikeri, one of our favourites being the river track to the spectacular Rainbow Falls.

Many of the islands that give the Bay its name fall within the Bay of Islands Maritime and Historic Park. Full details of the facilities and walking maps are available from the park headquarters in Russell or you can write to PO Box 134, Russell.

Because these areas are protected there are restrictions against pets, open fires and shooting. There are many species of wildlife and a dog or cat let loose could kill them. Similarly, one fire out of control could destroy the vegetation of a whole island and it would take years to grow again. If in doubt about the regulations please ask the rangers, who are there to help you enjoy the park.

During the Christmas holidays there is an organised holiday programme with activities such as guided walks, dinghy races and boat rallies (like a car rally on water). At that time of the year rangers patrol the Bay in runabouts and if you want information just wave them down.

If your cruising time is limited and you want to see as many of the islands as possible, take a trip on one of the commercial ferry boats. The Cream Trip is known throughout the world and is very popular with tourists. It drops off supplies at bays with permanent residents. Alternatively there is the trip to the 'Hole in the Rock' near Cape Brett.

There are several operators offering day trips or fishing leaving from Paihia and Russell. You will find notices around the town advertising them, or enquire at the information office.

Russell

Chart No: 5122 Bay of Islands
Map No: NZMS 280 Bay of Islands

Facilities

 FUEL on wharf, service from Fullers office at land end of wharf.

 GAS BOTTLES refilled at hardware shop, first street on left from waterfront.

 WATER none; nearest supply at Opua or Te Hue Bay.

 STORES groceries, vegetables, butchers, chemist, post office, souvenir and craft shops, restaurants and coffee shops, ice-cream parlour, banks (short hours), hardware, fishing and marine supplies, garage.

 RUBBISH DISPOSAL in jumbo bin to left of wharf.

 TOILETS public toilets on waterfront going towards park headquarters. No public showers or laundry but facilities for hire at camping ground. Enquire at camp office.

 HARBOUR-MASTER Opua, telephone Paihia 27-516.

 TELEPHONE at post office, first corner on right after the waterfront.

 POLICE on waterfront.

 FIRST AID doctor in telephone directory.

 LOCAL RADIO Radio Northland 1026.

⭐ **RANGER** Bay of Islands Maritime and Historic Park Headquarters, The Strand, telephone Russell 37-685.

We really enjoy Russell. It is not too far to come back to when we are out cruising around the Bay and we can have our mail sent to the post office where it is held for us until we call in for supplies. There is always something to watch, such as the game-fishing boats returning with the day's catch, or tourists from all parts of the world.

Anchorage

The beach at Russell shelves steeply and consists of small pebbles. Because this shingle extends some way out it is best to anchor well off the beach where there is mud to hold the anchor. Besides, the inner part of the bay is taken up with swing moorings, one of which is used by Fullers for its Cream Trip vessel. This needs plenty of room to swing and we have seen people drop anchor near the mooring only to find that they have to move when the ferry comes back in the late afternoon. This mooring is in the lee of the northern headland and usually has a dinghy left on it. The wash from the ferries and game fishing boats creates quite a disturbance but it is quieter further out.

There is space for anchoring on both sides of the wharf but leave the centre clear for the ferries, especially the catamaran which needs plenty of room to manoeuvre. The land on which the town is sited provides a little shelter from the east but the anchorage is very exposed to the west and there is not much shelter from north and south.

Landing is either at the wharf, where there is a dinghy jetty, or on the beach, but be sure to pull dinghies well up because they tend to slide on the shingle. Boats can tie up along the wharf for a limited time to take on supplies and fuel, but keep clear of the ferry berths.

If you wish to get away from the regular commercial traffic there is another anchorage in Matauwhi Bay, just around the corner from Russell, but it is so full of swing moorings that it is hard to get in close enough to shelter from either the wind or the sea motion. However, it is only a short walk back to Russell.

The wharf and streets of Russell are well lit so it is easy to enter at night, and if you want to treat yourself to a night on the town you will have no difficulty finding your way back to your boat.

Launching ramps

There are two ramps, one at the northern end of The Strand, concrete to low water, and a high-tide-only ramp at Matauwhi Bay. Parking for cars and trailers is much better at the Matauwhi Bay ramp because they can be left in the parking area looked after by park rangers and there is plenty of room. The Strand parking area is fairly small.

Recreation

There is plenty to see and do in Russell once you have done your shopping and stocked up the boat.

Park headquarters

The Bay of Islands Maritime and Historic Park headquarters and visitor centre is the place to visit first because it will tell you all about the area. It is open daily from 8.30 a.m. to 5 p.m. There are displays showing the islands' flora and fauna and what to see and do in the park. An audio-visual presentation tells the history of the area and the

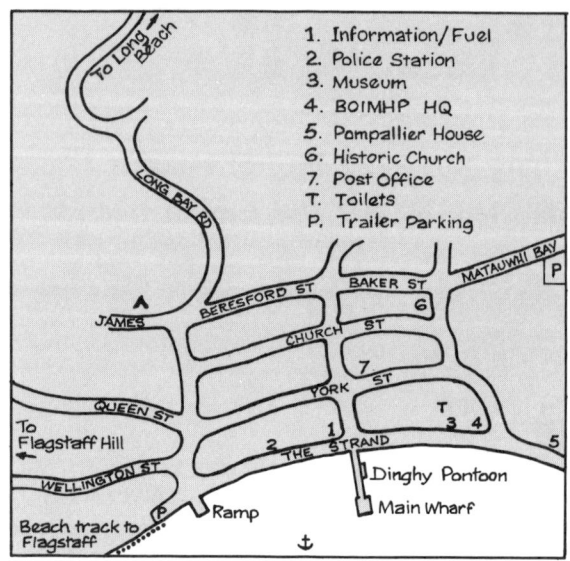

1. Information/Fuel
2. Police Station
3. Museum
4. BOIMHP HQ
5. Pompallier House
6. Historic Church
7. Post Office
T. Toilets
P. Trailer Parking

headquarters has a wide selection of books, pamphlets and photographs. It is situated along The Strand (the waterfront) to the right of the wharf. Entry is free.

Captain Cook Museum

Just across from the park headquarters is a little museum with relics of Russell's past. It is open seven days from 10 a.m. to 4 p.m. Admission is adults $1.50, children (5–14) 25 cents. Dogs are not admitted though there is a bowl of water for them at the door!

New Zealand's oldest church

Pompallier House

At the same end of The Strand is Pompallier House, built in 1841–42 as the printing house of the Catholic Mission of Bishop Pompallier, and later a private house. It now houses the original printing press and exhibits relating to the mission and early Kororareka.

It is administered by the Historic Places Trust. Entry is free to members of the Trust and the National Trusts of England, Scotland and Australia. For everyone else it is $2.50 adults, children (5–15) 50 cents. Opening hours are 10 a.m. to 12.30 p.m. and 1.30 p.m. to 4.30 p.m., shorter hours in winter. It is closed on Good Friday and Christmas Day.

These three places provide somewhere to pass an interesting wet day. If the weather is fine take a walk around Russell. You will see some of New Zealand's heritage such as Christ Church, New Zealand's oldest church, and the beautiful old building, now housing the police station, which was built in 1870.

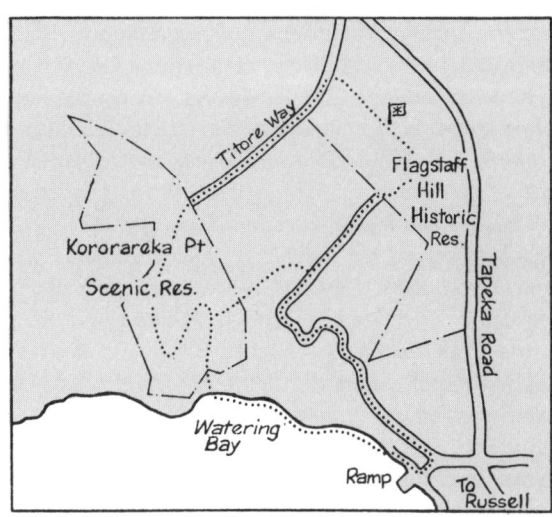

Pompallier House, Russell

Flagstaff Hill Historic Reserve

A steady 30-minute walk will take you up to Flagstaff Hill where there is a wonderful view over the Bay of Islands. If you are new to the area it is a good way to get your bearings. Across to the north-west you will see Kent Passage, one of the routes to Kerikeri.

There are three ways up to the top of Flagstaff Hill: along the beach from the boat ramp; via Wellington Street through some bush; and the route taken by cars. There are signposts at the northern end of Russell showing the way.

The walk is quite steep but just take it steady and you can rest on the seats at the top. A plaque at the foot of the flagstaff gives its history:

On this spot was erected in the year 1840 the first official signal flagstaff after the signing of the Treaty of Waitangi. Owing, however, to a misunderstanding between the two races the original flagstaff was cut down by the Maoris on July the 8th 1844 by one of Hone Heke's chiefs (he himself having pledged his word to Archdeacon William Williams not to cut it down as he had threatened, and on this occasion refused to break his word) and another having been erected in its place this in turn was cut down on January the 10th 1845. A third was erected on January the 17th and this was laid low before daylight on the 19th. This again was replaced by a fourth and this time sheathed for the lower 20 feet in iron as a future precaution. However, this proved no protection and the staff was again cut down in the early morning on March the 11th 1845. Kororareka was sacked and destroyed during the fighting which followed and this time the staff was not re-erected by the British.

However, during 1857 as a voluntary act of those who were directly concerned in cutting it down (and organised by Maihi Paraone Kawiti, son of Kawiti, one of the Maori chiefs) a noble spar was felled in the bush, towed to and prepared on the Kororareka beach, dragged up the hill by four hundred men specially chosen to represent every section of the Maori tribes no "friendly" being permitted part or lot in the undertaking.

For several weeks the band of willing workers toiled at their self-appointed task, and early in January 1858 the British flag, amidst the general rejoicing of both races, again floated at the peak of a mast which received the somewhat imposing title of "Whakakotahitanga" (being at one with the Queen) and through all the intervening years the peace which it commemorated has never been broken.

The present staff is the remaining portion of the original "Whakakotahitanga".

Russell Police Station

By the time you have digested this information and admired the view you will have recovered sufficiently to walk back into Russell. Take an alternative route and once back in Russell you can reward your effort with an ice-cream, cup of tea or coffee, or something a little stronger if the tavern is open. The Duke of Marlborough Hotel, the first hotel to hold a liquor licence in New Zealand, is on the waterfront.

Opua

Chart No: 5123 Approaches to Opua and Opua Wharf

Map No: NZMS 280 Bay of Islands

Facilities

 FUEL on Opua store wharf to right of main wharf.

 GAS/KEROSENE at store.

 WATER several taps on main wharf.

 STORES groceries, take-aways, chandlery, garage, fresh fish from Pearl Fisheries on wharf.

 RUBBISH DISPOSAL in bin at seaward end of main wharf.

 TOILETS public toilets.

 SHOWERS behind wharf end of Cruising Club; 50 cents.

 LAUNDRY at store.

 HARBOUR-MASTER P. Sharp, telephone Paihia 27-516, office at end of wharf.

 TELEPHONE outside Cruising Club.

 REPAIRS there are several boat yards at Opua which provide haul-out facilities and repairs. There is also a grid for hull cleaning in front of the Harbour Board office.

 POWER power points on the main wharf. For long-term use make arrangements with the harbour-master. There is no charge for short jobs.

 POSTAL agency – see below.

Anchorage

Opua is one of the Ports of Entry for overseas boats. There is a clearance fee of $50 for these boats, which includes one night's berthage at the main wharf, power, water and a shower.

Other visitors may use the wharf for loading or unloading without charge but if you need to be alongside the wharf for an extended period please arrange with the harbour-master. The charge is $6.60 per day.

Swing moorings are available to rent from the Harbour Board if you are staying for any length of time. For short visits there is space to anchor, but the anchorage is not very protected as the rivers Waikare and Kawakawa meet the Veronica Channel at Opua and there is a tidal flow of up to three knots.

There is a dinghy landing stage on the inside of the main wharf. Landing along the shore is not advisable.

The vehicular ferry for cars travelling to and from Russell runs from Opua so be sure to keep clear of its berth to the right of the main wharf.

Launching ramp

There is a concrete ramp to low water, formerly a ferry ramp. However, parking for cars and trailers is not good. There is some space along the riverside but be careful how you park as the Bay of Islands Scenic Railway stops here.

Recreation

Opua is a base for overseas yachts riding out the Pacific cyclone season, and for repairs. However, it is worth a visit if you are having a holiday in the Bay and there is a good long walk to stretch cramped legs, and a train ride for fun.

Opua-Paihia Walkway
This walk is 8 km long and takes about three hours. If you have a large enough crew on board perhaps some could walk and the rest take the boat to Paihia to meet them. Children can work off some of their energy, but dogs are not allowed on the walk.

From the wharf the walk follows the coastline by a path to Cherry Bay, used since early days. Continuing on to the Harrison Scenic Reserve the track climbs slightly to a navigation beacon. From here a side track leads to a vantage point on the Veronica Point subdivision.

Opua Store

Around Veronica Point a boardwalk crosses an inlet allowing a close look at the ecology of the mangroves and the habitat of the banded rail. Past the motor camp and around the next point the walk continues along the causeway. Except at high tide the shoreline is followed again to Stockyard Point at the southern end of Paihia. At high tide the main road gives access. There is a short walk up to the Stockyard Point Scenic Reserve and a picnic area.

Steam train at Opua

Bay of Islands Scenic Railway
This is a steam train journey of about two hours which runs from Opua along the Waikare Inlet through tunnels and over bridges to the town of Kawakawa. The train then runs through the main shopping street, a novelty for both passengers and onlookers. It is a fun trip for all ages and there is a half-hour stop in Kawakawa for shopping and refreshments.

The train has open or closed carriages pulled by a Pickett steam-engine. In summer the train runs daily at 10 a.m. and 2 p.m., with a reduced timetable in winter.

Opua Cruising Club
The clubhouse of the Opua Cruising Club is at the shore end of the wharf and the club welcomes members of other boating clubs. Opening hours are Wednesday nights and weekends with longer hours in the summer if members are available to run it. Members are pleased to help visiting boaties with local knowledge.

Crews of the large contingent of overseas boats

Opua dinghy wharf

that visit Opua from December to April use the clubhouse as their base and arrange lectures on boating topics, instruction and examination for radio licences and social activities such as a 'turkey dinner'. The crews contact each other on VHF Channel 8 at 8 a.m. each day to find out about activities.

Opua Regatta
The Opua Regatta is held in mid-January on the Saturday with the nearest high tide to 2 p.m. There are stalls along the wharf selling second-hand boating gear, crafts and food, and on the water there are dinghy races and yacht racing organised by the Opua Cruising Club. Club members serve delicious morning and afternoon teas in the clubhouse.

Opua Postal Agency
For many years this little office underneath the Harbour Board has been a friend to sailors from all over the world. Mail can be held here. It has now changed from a post office to a postal agency which means that such services as banking have been discontinued. However, it continues to handle all mail facilities together with the sale of postcards,

greeting cards and stationery. There is also a book and magazine exchange, photocopying and fax machines, and a booking agency for Clark's Northliner coaches, which provide transport for passengers and freight between Auckland and Northland.

Paihia

Just up the coast from Opua is Paihia. Unfortunately Paihia is not very sheltered for an anchorage and in places is very shallow. But it does have a larger range of shops than either Opua or Russell so it may be worth a visit in settled weather to stock up.

Details of leisure activities in Paihia are available from the Public Relations Office on the waterfront. Worth a visit are the Shipwreck Museum in a three-masted barque moored alongside the Waitangi Bridge, and the Waitangi National Reserve, including the Treaty House, Maori meeting house and war canoe.

Paihia is a tourist centre so has plenty of eating places for refreshment and motels and hotels for accommodation.

Kerikeri

Chart No: 5122 Bay of Islands
Map No: NZMS 280 Bay of Islands

Facilities

Most facilities and services are in the main township, which is about a kilometre and a half from the Stone Store. Fortunately it is downhill on the way back, when you will be loaded up with stores. There are plenty of coffee shops for refreshments before your walk back.

 FUEL at Stone Store Basin, service from Stone Store.

 GAS BOTTLES refilled at Caltex garage by roundabout at end of main shops and also Mill Lane industrial area.

 KEROSENE at hardware store and garage.

 WATER tap on wharf.

 STORES all kinds of stores, including a large supermarket, post office, banks, sports shops, hardware, clothing and books. The Stone Store sells ice-creams and a limited range of groceries, such as butter and milk, but no bread.

 RUBBISH DISPOSAL there is a bin beside the wharf.

 TOILETS public toilets in the parking and picnic area over the bridge from the Stone Store.

 SHOWERS/LAUNDRY there are no showers or laundry for boaties by the anchorage but it is sometimes possible to use

 the laundry at the Aranga Holiday Park, just past the shopping centre, depending on the demand from resident users. Telephone 79-326 to enquire.

 HARBOUR-MASTER Bill Franklin, telephone 79-028.

 TELEPHONE at post office or across the road from the wharf (take a torch if using at night as there is no light). There is no directory either so you will have to call the operator if you do not have the number required.

 POLICE main road just before the shops start, telephone Kerikeri 79-211.

 FIRST AID see telephone book for doctors, dentists and vets.

 REPAIRS there is a good selection of chandlery at the hardware store and various repair facilities in the Mill Lane industrial area including a sailmaker. Kerikeri Cruising Club grid at Doves Bay is available for hire. Book at Crawfords Hardware, telephone Kerikeri 77-420.

 MARINE RADIO Kerikeri Radio listening on VHF channel 16, SSB 2480 or 4419.4.

 TRANSPORT buses to Auckland and Northland depart from outside the travel agents in Cobham Road, opposite the rugby club. Domestic air service from Kerikeri airport.

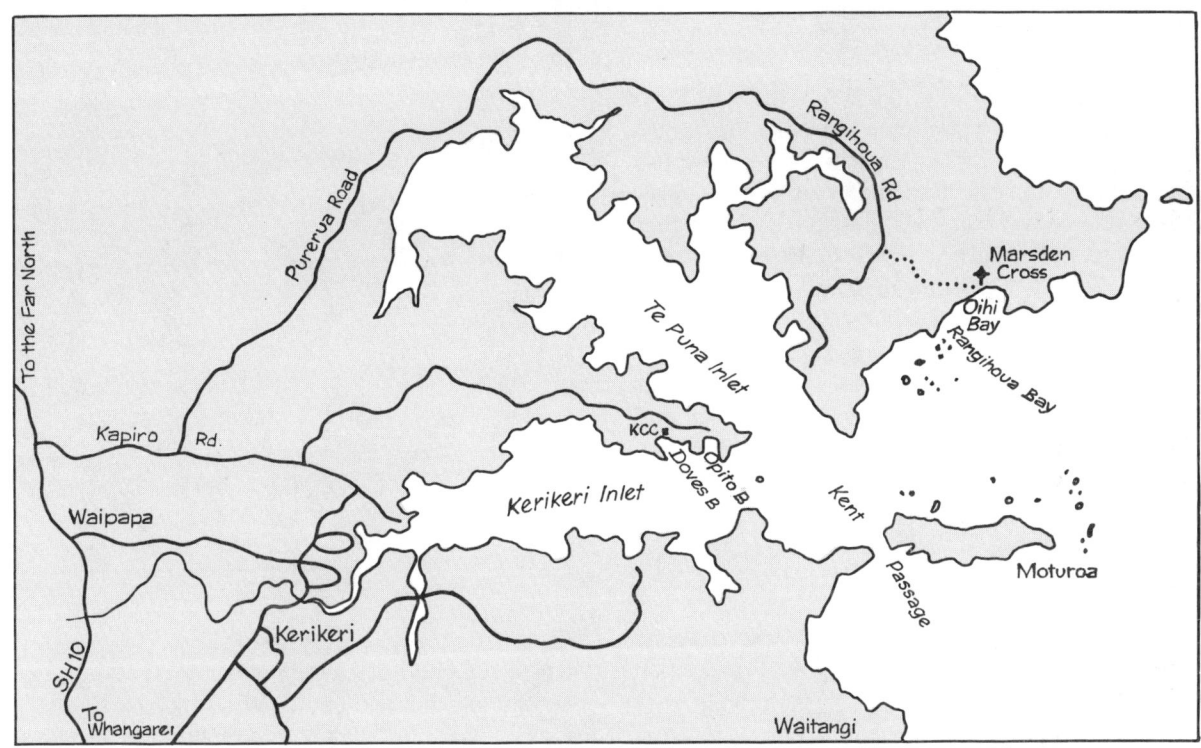

Getting to Kerikeri

Kerikeri can only be reached by deep-draught boats an hour either side of the high tide – at one point there is only a few centimetres of water at low tide! However, the channel is well marked so just follow the markers at a steady speed.

If the tide is not at a convenient level when you arrive at the entrance both Opito and Doves Bay provide good waiting anchorages. We usually use Opito because there are fewer moorings and there is a good beach for landing.

On leaving Doves or Opito keep to the same side of the inlet and look in the distance for an island and some moorings. You will then see one red and two green beacons to starboard of the island. This is the start of the channel and from here on you can see the markers. There is another channel on the other side of the river from Doves and Opito so do not get the markers for that channel confused. *Pickmere's Atlas* shows the navigation very clearly.

If you are going up in the evening be careful because the light of the setting sun shines on the water and obscures the outer mooring buoys, which are very near the channel. One of these round the propeller would not be much help. The same care must be taken when coming out of the river in the early morning into the glare of the rising sun.

Eventually you reach a signpost indicating the Stone Store Basin to port and Waipapa Landing to starboard.

Owners of shallow-draught boats should check the chart to see what stage of the tide suits their own boat. We are talking from experience of our own 1.7 m draught and find one hour before high tide ideal.

Anchorage

There is very little room for anchoring in the Stone Store Basin. Most visitors use the poles, which cost $3.30 per day or $20 per week. This can be arranged through Kerikeri Radio. Call them on VHF Channel 16 before making the trip up the river and they will check with the harbour-master which pole berth is available.

Keep to the channel in the Basin and do not go further than the last starboard hand marker except to use the wharf. There are patches of boulders and many areas dry out. Landing is easy at the well-maintained wharf with plenty of space for dinghies to be tied to the railings – it sometimes looks like the equivalent of a shore car-park!

The Basin is very sheltered with a high bank on either side. However, after really heavy rain the water rushes down the river and sometimes brings logs with it. This is another reason for not recommending anchoring.

Yachts should use the wharf at high tide to take on fuel and water. Launches have more flexibility.

Launching ramp

There is a ramp at Waipapa Landing with concrete to low water and good parking. The river forks when it has almost reached Kerikeri – one branch goes to the Stone Store Basin and the other to Waipapa Landing.

Opito Bay, at the seaward end of Kerikeri inlet, also has a concrete ramp with good parking.

Recreation

Kerikeri has many beautiful walks. However, most are part of the Bay of Islands Maritime and Historic Park, so no dogs are allowed. If you have a dog, exercise it at the domain in the centre of Kerikeri,

Kerikeri inlet

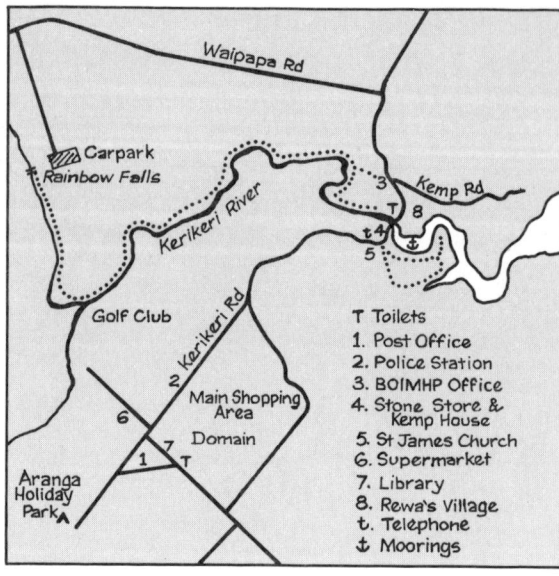

T Toilets
1. Post Office
2. Police Station
3. BOIMHP Office
4. Stone Store & Kemp House
5. St James Church
6. Supermarket
7. Library
8. Rewa's Village
t. Telephone
↨ Moorings

which is a good place for ball games. There is also an empty subdivision at the end of Kemp Road – the first road on the right over the bridge – where dogs can have a good run around away from traffic and suburban gardens.

Rainbow Falls

Not far from the township are the 27 m-high Rainbow Falls which get their name from the Maori word waiaaniwaniwa, meaning waters of the rainbow. The falls can be reached either by road – along the Waipapa road and turn off where signposted – or on foot along a lovely riverside walk which is suitable for all ages.

The walk starts from the car-park across the bridge from the Stone Store. At first the track is across open meadow with the river to one side. There is plenty of space for children to run around, and picnic tables so you can have a meal away from the boat for a change.

The track then enters a wooded area with much of the path made of natural boulders. The path goes up and down but is not steep. However, good shoes are needed in wet weather as it can be slippery. There is a side track to the Wharepuke Falls, then the track passes orchards, Kerikeri's main industry. Allow one and a half hours each way.

Another interesting short walk starts on the left

Stone Store Basin, Kerikeri

just past the Stone Store tea-rooms and goes to an historic pa site. There is a good view of the river from here.

Details of other walks can be obtained from the ranger's office on the left-hand side of the road across the bridge near the playcentre and Scout den.

Kemp House

Kemp House and the Stone Store belonged to a settlement established by the Church Missionary Society in 1819 under the protection of Hongi Hika and Rewa. The timber-constructed Kemp House is the oldest surviving colonial building in New Zealand. It was erected in 1821–22 for the Rev. John Butler, but the Butlers left Kerikeri in 1823 and the house was taken over by George and Martha Clarke.

In 1832 it was assigned to the lay missionary and mission blacksmith James Kemp. When James, his wife, Charlotte, and their many children moved in the Kemps began an association with the house that was to last for more than 140 years. His descendants presented it to the New Zealand Historic Places Trust in 1974.

Hand-forged nails made by Kemp can be seen in the construction of the house and it is furnished with the Kemp furniture brought from England, including the dining table, which breaks down so it can be transported in a ship's cabin.

The garden was washed away in the flood of 1981 and the present garden is based on what research has revealed of the garden in missionary times. One survivor of the flood was the special rose Slater's Crimson China, which blooms continuously. It is reputed to have been planted by Samuel Butler, son of the Rev. John Butler, in the 1820s.

Kemp House is open to the public 10 a.m. to 12.30 p.m. and 1.30 p.m. to 4.30 p.m. daily except Christmas Day and Good Friday, with reduced opening hours in winter. Admission is adults $2.50, children 50 cents, members of the Trust free.

Stone Store

The Stone Store is the oldest stone building in New Zealand and was erected in 1832–36 to store the supplies of the Church Missionary Society. Today it is the property of the New Zealand Historic Places Trust but still operates as a store. There is also a museum upstairs, admission $1.

St James Anglican Church

St James Anglican Church, an attractive wooden building, up the hill from the Stone Store, was part of the mission. The present building was erected in 1878 on the site of an earlier chapel.

Rewa's village

Just over the bridge from the Stone Store to the right

is a replica of a Maori village. It was built to demonstrate the Maori presence in the area before the founding of the mission in 1819. Admission is adults $1, children 20 cents.

Sports

Golf – Kerikeri Golf Club is easily reached from the Stone Store Basin. It is in Golf View Road which is at the end of Fairway Drive. Visitors are welcome and clubs are available for hire. The club is open every day and the bar is open 3 p.m. to 6.30 p.m. on weekends.

Tennis – Courts in Cobham Road just along from the shopping centre.

Swimming pool – A public pool is in Hone Heke Road, the first road on the left walking towards the township from the Stone Store Basin.

Kerikeri Cruising Club

Kerikeri Cruising Club members welcome visitors to their lovely modern clubhouse in Doves Bay. During the summer it is open 9 a.m.–5.30 p.m. from a week before Christmas to the end of January. A custodian is in attendance to provide morning and afternoon teas and information. Showers are available for 50 cents.

On Boxing Day the club hosts the Royal New Zealand Yacht Squadron and on New Year's Day it runs a Round the Islands Race. Visiting boats are welcome to take part – be at Doves Bay by 10 a.m. to enter – and the day ends with a barbecue and band and the club bar is open.

A cleaning grid is available for hire at a charge of $5 per day for non-members. Book through Crawfords Hardware, telephone Kerikeri 77-420. If you require the temporary use of a mooring this can probably be arranged through the club.

Other entertainment

Kerikeri is most famous for its fruit growing – primarily citrus but increasingly newer crops of kiwifruit, persimmons, tamarillos, avocados and macadamia nuts. There are orchards along every road in Kerikeri where you can buy fruit, so the crew should be safe from scurvy. Some orchards are open to the public, but these are further out of town and if you have arrived by boat they are too far to reach on foot.

Craft shops are plentiful as many artistic people live and sell their work in Kerikeri.

A good shop for a rainy day is the Kerikeri Bargain Centre which sells all sorts of novelties, books, games and gifts. There is also a book swap to renew your holiday reading. For more sophisticated reading there is a very cosy reading room in the library and if you are staying for some time in Kerikeri a visitor's library card is available for $10. The library is open all day Monday, Wednesday and Friday and mornings only on Tuesday, Thursday and Saturday.

If you plan a night on the town take a torch for your walk back to the basin as there is no street lighting out of the town. The basin itself is well lit with a light on the wharf and spotlights on Kemp House.

Roberton Island

Roberton Island

Also known by its Maori name, Motuarohia, this is the first island after Fraser Rocks at the tip of the peninsula on which Russell stands. It is a good day trip from Russell or a first stop if you have just picked up a charter yacht.

The main anchorage is on the south side of the island. The bay is wide with plenty of room and good landing for dinghies or runabouts on a sandy beach. The island itself is steep so provides shelter from the north-west to north-east, but if the wind is strong it may funnel through breaks in the land.

Underwater Trail

One of the attractions of Roberton Island is the Underwater Trail set up by the Bay of Islands Maritime and Historic Park, the first in New Zealand.

It is in the natural lagoon and numbered signs mark items of interest in the water. For young children who cannot swim the trail can be followed at half tide and below.

Signs are in place from Christmas to Easter and a pamphlet explaining the trail is available. In case you cannot get a copy we will reprint the details here. The trail is to be followed clockwise.

Kelpfish (1) are often seen in small groups of three or four perched on rocks or in narrow cracks beneath the kelp forest. However, it is not a herbivore. The little kelpie lurks here waiting for unsuspecting marine life such as a passing blenny or small crab to pounce on. Big Eye (3) are typically found schooling in places like this cave by day. Yet at night these small fish come out of hiding to feed as individuals.

Seaweeds are the forests of the ocean. There are many species of kelp, both large and small, much like plants ashore. Neptune's necklace (2) is invariably short with many lengths of nobbly beads. However, Ecklonia radiata (4) is quite the opposite − its branchless trunks can grow quite tall before the crown divides into many flattened straps. Both have hold-fasts which secure the plants to the sea floor so that wave action does not wash them away.

Much of what you already know about nature applies in the sea. For example, trees and seaweed both have trunks and leaves. They also provide food and shelter for many other animals.

It is a useful technique to compare things you know with those you don't, looking for similarities and differences. Why not try it? Cushion Stars (5) are common and extremely variable in colour. Green, black, orange and blue versions have all been seen. A good test of your observational skills is to see how many stars of each colour can be found.

Kina (sea eggs) and starfish are closely related. There are common features which help to identify them as members of the same family. Radial symmetry is one such feature which is readily identifiable in cushion stars, especially when looking at the animals' undersides. This species and other starfish exhibit five-sided symmetry which is also common to the kina. Next time you find the test (shell) of a dead kina have a close look for five-sided symmetry.

Blennies are probably the most common fish in the lagoon. They are mostly long (not more than 10 cm), slender fish which generally hug the bottom. The crested blenny (6) lives in holes. Often all that can be seen is part of the head crowned by its distinctive crest. When these fish are out swimming a dark stripe from the eye to the tail is also very noticeable. The banded blenny (7) is conspicuous by its bright colouring. The alternating bands are brown and white but the clearest distinguishing feature is the bright blue eyes unique to this species.

The mottled blenny's clearest distinguishing feature is the six mottly (incomplete) vertical bands. Blennies are carnivorous; small crabs are often on the menu but most chance titbits that pass their way are tested.

Kina, as previously mentioned, are closely related to starfish but there are many other observable features. Spines and tube feet are readily seen on both sea eggs and (11) armed and comb stars. Both animals depend on their tube feet for locomotion. However, the starfish also use them to grasp and pull apart the two shells of bivalves (for example, scallops). Once the shells are opened the soft animal is at the mercy of the starfish.

Food chains are an ecological concept familiar to most. Humorous and often inaccurate versions have been popularised in folk songs, such as '. . . the horse which ate the cow which ate the cat which ate the mouse which ate the spider which ate the fly . . .' However, food chains are the very essence of life.

If you stand still long enough in the lagoon you may develop a tickling sensation round your legs. Closer observation usually reveals shrimps swarming like sandflies. The miniature pincers of these shrimps are pecking at flaking dead skin and are completely harmless.

Although small, these creatures make up in numbers what they lack in size. In fact they are one of the most numerous species in the pool. If shrimps were the size of their close relations the crayfish and prawn, many gatherers of kaimoana (seafood) would be very happy.

Leatherjackets (13) are not clothed in a coarse mat of overlapping scales like snapper or most other bony fish. These fish have a tough leathery skin with tiny scales which when touched feel like sandpaper. Leatherjackets use their chisel-like teeth to nibble and nip at sponges and other encrusting life from rocks.

If you notice a blenny-like fish seeming to swim around with sunglasses on then you have found the spectacled blenny. Like most of the blenny family it does not grow large and uses camouflage as protection.

Many different species of sponges live in and around the pool; one of the most interesting is the golf ball sponge (15). The golf ball sponge is a little larger than its namesake and perhaps not quite the right colour (often orange), but its even, spherical shape and dimples suggest an amazing similarity.

Crabs are feared by some. Large pincers and threatening poses are designed to strike fear into potential attackers, humans included. But it's an act of bravado. Most crabs seem to hold that 'he who scuttles away lives to fight another day' The red rock crab (16) and its relative the shrimp live the life of scavengers. The pincers are rarely used to grasp or kill prey.

Spotties (17, 18) exhibit characteristics which are unusual to say the least and not observed on land. For example, all spotties begin life as females and it is not until adulthood and the opportunity to exist as an adult that males develop. Juveniles and females have a single large black blotch just beneath the dorsal fin while males have several small black blotches.

Seaweeds can be divided into three main groups, browns, greens and reds. Comb weed (19) is a red seaweed rich in agar. The agar is often used in laboratories as a culture medium.

Some of the larger fish, such as the parore, are usually only noticeable at high tide when they arrive in greater numbers. Largely grazers, these fish move on to the shallow beds to feed during high tide.

A good test of your skills of observation and identification is to set yourself targets. For example, how many species of crab or seaweed can you find?

After you have done the Trail you could take a walk up through the pine trees to the look-out on top of the hill at the western end of the beach. From here there is a good view out over the Bay and back down over the lagoon. If you have children with you, do not let them get too far ahead as there is a steep drop over the cliff on the other side of the island.

The swimming in the bay is good with clear water and a good beach for children. If you want to picnic there is shade under the pine trees on the hill.

There are no facilities of any kind on Roberton, and since it is part of the Maritime and Historic Park no pets can be taken ashore.

Moturua Scenic Reserve

Moturua Island

This island is next to Roberton to the east and has several anchorages giving shelter in most winds, and sandy beaches for runabouts to land. There are no facilities such as toilets or water.

Most of the island is administered by the Bay of Islands Maritime and Historic Park, but there is some private land on the southern part of the island. A marked walkway circles the island and you will find pamphlets in a box beside the marker showing the entry points to the walk.

Moturua has been used by many people for different reasons. Captain Cook landed at Waipao or Frenchmens Bay on the south-west side in 1769 and the *Endeavour*'s water casks were filled from the stream. Three years later the French arrived, led by Marion du Fresne. They were on an exploration of the South Pacific but the ships needed repairs and some of the men were sick so they set up camp on the island.

Unfortunately du Fresne and two boat-loads of his men were killed on a trip to the mainland. In revenge the French killed many of the Maori, then left New Zealand, leaving behind a claim to this country buried in a bottle. It has never been found.

Waipao Bay used to have a watering buoy, but it has been removed so anyone with old information should be warned that no water is available on Moturua.

The island has been used for cultivation and farming and now the regenerating native forest is being encouraged. Species already emerging in wetter areas include mahoe, whau, kawakawa and tree fern, and young pohutukawa abound along the coast.

The anchorage we prefer is on the south-east side. We know it as Norwegian Bay (in 1912 a Norwegian whaling expedition made the island its headquarters), but it has other names. There are two

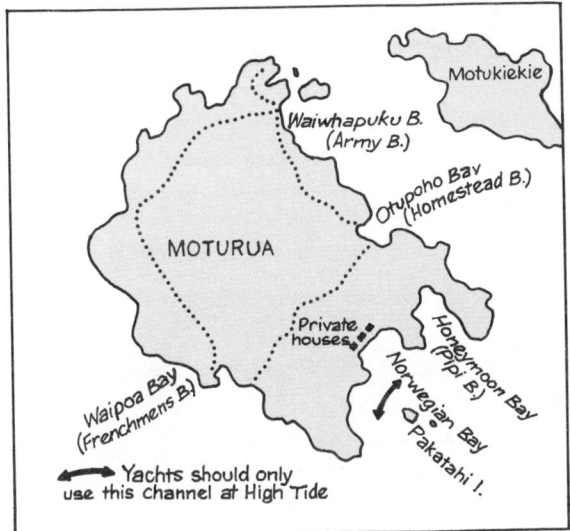

Yachts should only use this channel at High Tide

parts to the bay divided by Pakatahi Island, so another name for it is Twin Bay.

For yachts the deepest part is the right-hand side of the bay with the houses. Yachts can pass between Pakatahi and Moturua at high tide but, at other times, go around the marker at the southern end of Pakatahi. The left-hand side of the bay has no houses and a lovely sandy beach for a game. This is the only part of the island where dogs can land or be exercised as the rest of the island is part of the Maritime and Historic Park.

Pakatahi Island is a good spot for fishing. We have had many a delicious snapper dinner as a result of dropping a line over the side here.

Just around the corner is Pipi or Honeymoon Bay. According to the ferry boat captains it is so called because the beach is so small there is only room for two! It certainly is small but the bay itself provides good shelter as it is long and narrow with steep sides. However, it does get very crowded and the proximity to the land allows bugs to get aboard. Mosquitoes and crickets were a problem when we visited. We have also heard of people being plagued by wasps.

During the Christmas holiday period there is a rubbish barge off the south-east corner of Moturua Island just around from Honeymoon Bay.

Further around on the east side are two more bays – Otupoho Bay (Homestead Bay) and Waiwhapuku Bay (Army Bay). Homestead is more sheltered than Army Bay for overnight anchoring as a swell comes in between Moturua and the next island, Motukiekie. However, Army Bay has a nice beach with a few trees for shade and links up with the walk around the island.

A short walk takes you up the path to the headland to the right of the beach. There are good views and if you are planning to make the passage between the islands for the first time it is a good way to see the rocks from above. It looks quite frightening from sea-level, but an aerial view puts it into perspective!

Army Bay is so called because during World War II minefields were laid in the Bay of Islands and this spot was the control base with housing and camp facilities. The buildings have now been removed but some evidence still remains. This is the sort of place for the young members of the crew to use their imaginations and get rid of some of their energy.

Urupukapuka Island Recreation Reserve

Paradise Bay, Urupukapuka Island

This is the largest island in the Bay of Islands and has facilities for camping. There is also a very interesting five-hour archaeological walk around the island.

Neither Cook nor du Fresne visited Urupukapuka. A whaling captain named Brind claimed to have bought 150 acres from the Ngapuhi chief Rewa in 1839 for a mare valued at 45 pounds, but the claim was not upheld. In the later 1800s two Europeans, Greenway and Symonds, leased some land on the island for grazing. In 1905 the land was partitioned into shares for 98 claimants and soon after Mr Baker of Russell began to buy up the land from the Maori shareholders.

In 1927 Otehei Bay became known throughout the world when the American writer Zane Grey made it a base for fishing expeditions.

The island was acquired for the public in 1971 and, apart from a few pieces of private land, belongs to the Bay of Islands Maritime and Historic Park.

There are no good anchorages on the northern coast, but there are three on the west side for shelter from the north round to the east – Otiao (Indico) Bay, Oneura (Paradise) Bay and Otehei Bay, and Urupukapuka Bay on the east side for protection from south-west to north. Note the wharf in Otehei Bay is for use by the scheduled ferry trips only, but if you wish to land people for camping please make prior arrangements with the caretaker, telephone Russell 37-803.

Cable Bay, just round the corner from Otehei Bay, is also a good spot as some protection is provided by the islands off the southern point. This is a popular beach with runabouts, which come across from the mainland. The beaches are sandy and good for landing. However, once ashore there is not much shade from the sun, so take some protection if you have sensitive skin.

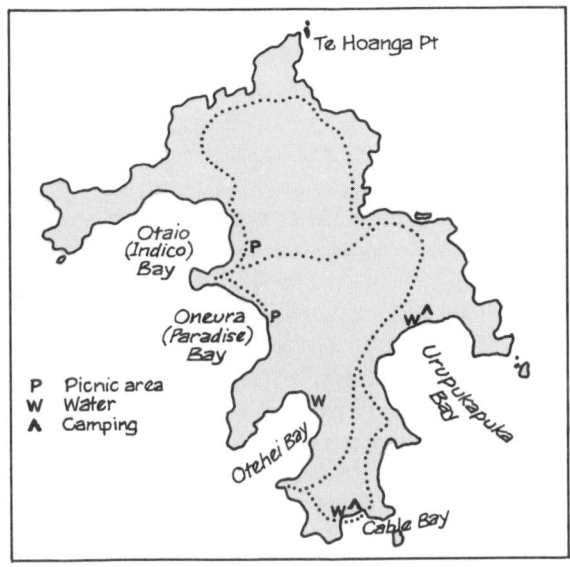

P   Picnic area
W   Water
⋏   Camping

Archaeological walk

Two centuries before the crew of the *Endeavour* became the first Europeans to enter the Bay of Islands, a thriving Maori community lived on Urupukapuka. They were a sub-tribe of the Ngaare Raumati, who occupied the south-east Bay of Islands. The very first settlers of Urupukapuka, distant ancestors of the modern Maori, may have arrived here around 1000 years ago.

Very little is known or recorded about pre-European life on Urupukapuka so the best record of the past is provided by numerous archaeological sites visible on the present day landscape. By interpreting these sites it is possible to see into the daily lives of ancient communities.

Pamphlets showing the route are available from the park headquarters and from boxes at entry points.

The walk takes about five hours and is designed to be done in a clockwise direction. If you do not want to do the whole walk there are two sections of two and a half hours each, or you can walk some of the path from the entry points at different bays.

The southern loop covers more sites and overlooks calm, sheltered bays. The northern loop visits fewer sites but includes some of the more interesting and spectacular and there are dramatic views from high rugged cliffs – keep an eye on the children!

Some of the walk is across open ground – in some parts sheep are grazing – and some through bush. We found the path difficult to find from Oneura Bay but Cyclone Bola had just caused considerable storm damage and fallen trees could

Cable Bay, Urupukapuka Island

have been obscuring the path.

A good view of Albert Channel can be obtained from the top of the headland at the right-hand side of Urupukapuka Bay. We find it helps to see hazards from above before negotiating them at sea-level.

Don't forget, this is part of the Maritime and Historic Park so no dogs or cats are allowed.

Urupukapuka

Camping

Camping on Urupukapuka is intended for those seeking a 'back to nature' camping experience relying on their own resources. The informal camping is made possible by combining farming with recreation. As the grazing of the island reduces the fire risk, one can pitch a tent almost anywhere. However, camping is not allowed in the privately leased Otehei Bay or Indico and Paradise Bays, which are set aside for day visitors.

This camping facility is ideal for people with runabouts or day sailers who do not have much room on board. If you have a trailer boat you can leave your car and trailer in the car-park at Rawhiti on the mainland where for a small charge it will be looked after for you. Launching is from the beach.

The most popular sites are Urupukapuka Bay and Cable Bay. Water and open-air showers are provided for campers at these bays. Boaties are asked to get their water from the watering barge in Otehei Bay — to starboard as you approach the wharf.

Fires are not permitted. Campers must have a portable gas or liquid fuel stove. There are no toilets. Either take a portable chemical toilet or a spade to dig a hole. Spades can be hired from the park headquarters.

Charges are $3 per site per night (two adults, children under 15 years free), $1.50 per night for each additional adult. You must register on arrival at the registration booth in either Cable Bay or Urupukapuka Bay, or with the ranger who visits the island daily or at the park headquarters in Russell. Camping is only allowed on a pre-paid basis.

Rubbish must be removed from the island so take plenty of bags. It can be taken to the barge moored off Moturua.

Manawaora Bay

Te Hue water jetty

While the Bay of Islands is best known for the islands which give it its name, there are many good anchorages on the mainland. To the east of Russell is Manawaora Bay, which includes Orokawa Bay, Te Hue Bay, Opunga Cove and Jacks Bay.

Orokawa Bay

Orokawa is a long sandy beach on the southern side of a peninsula running from east to west. It provides good shelter from the north, the higher land at either end of the beach giving the most shelter. The anchorage has good holding close in with easy landing on the beach for dinghies or runabouts. There are trees at both ends of the beach to provide shade from the sun and there is plenty of room for children to play.

There are some houses on the beach and sheep graze on the open grass, but it is not park land so you can take your dog ashore provided it is kept on a lead to prevent it chasing the sheep and running into private gardens.

A short walk across the peninsula takes you to the beach on the more exposed northern coast, where conditions can be quite different. One day when the water was flat calm in the anchorage we walked across to the other side to find large rollers breaking on the beach.

Te Hue Bay

Te Hue Bay is tucked in further along the peninsula and is the source of the best water in the Bay of Islands. Thanks to the generosity of one of the local landowners, Dave Smith, boaties are able to tie up to a good wharf and take on water. A donation towards the upkeep of the wharf is requested and this can be left in the box on the wharf.

The residents of this bay have not always been so friendly. A monument on the top of the cliff reveals it was here that Marion du Fresne and some of his men were murdered in 1772.

The bay itself is not very big and there are hidden rocks by the wharf so do not go in too close. It is best to take on water at or near high tide to give yourself plenty of room to manoeuvre. It is a good anchorage in certain conditions but there is more room in nearby Opunga Cove.

Opunga Cove

Opunga Cove is sheltered on all sides except north-west. It was here that we and ten other boats spent a week riding out Cyclone Bola in March 1988. None of us dragged our anchor – although some did use two anchors.

During one 24-hour spell we were unable to get ashore because it was too rough to launch the dinghy, but apart from that we were better off than the people on the shore. There are some holiday homes in Opunga Cove and the residents were without power (including the facility to pump water from the tanks) and telephone and the road was closed by fallen trees. On our boat in the bay we had our gas stove, kerosene lights, full water tanks in the bilge and radio-telephone communication with the rest of the world. We also had plenty of supplies as boaties usually stock up well for such emergencies.

The wind during Bola was from the south-east.

At the end of the cyclone it changed direction round to the north and blew straight in to the bay so we all made the short trip across to Orokawa, which was totally sheltered. The anchor was difficult to get out, which proves there is good holding in Opunga Cove.

Opunga Cove has a sandy beach in the middle and rocky cliffs either side with interesting rock pools at low tide. At low tide pipis can be found in the sand. The land on which the houses are built is privately owned and there is no access to the beach from the road for the general public. However, the beach is public land and dogs can go ashore here provided they are kept under control.

Jacks Bay

Jacks Bay, where the Jack and Jill Beach Resort is situated, is another good bay in Manawaora Bay. For many years the management of the resort were not friendly towards boaties, but it has now changed hands and the present owners could not have been more helpful when we called in. Facilities available to boaties include use of showers, laundry, a well-stocked camp store, telephone, boat ramp and dive air filling. There is also a rubbish trailer, the philosophy of the new owners being that it is better to have boaties' rubbish in the trailer than floating out in the bay and spoiling it for everyone!

If you want friends to meet you for a day out on the boat they can leave their car here for a small fee and there are camp and caravan sites, cabins and motel units if they want to stay.

The roll that comes in from the north can make landing in the dinghy a bit tricky at times, but if you are desperate for a hot shower or a cold ice-cream, it is a small price to pay.

Parekura Bay

This is a large bay on the mainland beside the road to Rawhiti. It is useful as a contact point if you want to pick up friends when you are out cruising in the Bay. It is also near the start of the walk to Whangamumu Harbour on the east coast.

The upper reaches of the separate bays dry out so do not go in too far. A good anchorage for a south-westerly (the prevailing wind) is in the lee of the cliffs in Te Uenga Bay. There are some permanent moorings but there is still room for a few boats to anchor.

One of our cruising guides says Waipiro Bay is good in westerly winds, but in such a wind we found it was funnelling down over the land making the anchorage very unpleasant. Because of the shallow nature of the bay it is not possible to get close enough to the land to be protected from the wind.

At Te Uenga a sandy beach provides good landing and there is road access to the beach. There are no shops or facilities in the bay apart from rubbish bins on the main road just up from the beach. A walk along the road is a good way to stretch boat-cramped legs and there are some good views over the Bay.

Just around from Parekura Bay is Omakiwi Cove, a sandy beach sheltered from most winds except westerlies.

If you want to take the walk over to Whangamumu the start of the track is well signposted on the Rawhiti road (to the left/east from Parekura) and there is a parking area for vehicles. It takes about one hour each way through native bush with good views of the coast. The bay is good for swimming and picnics, so makes a pleasant day outing. Whangamumu has fresh water but no toilets or other facilities. Further details about the anchorage are in the coastal section.

Rawhiti

House on Rawhiti Rd – start of Cape Brett Walk

Rawhiti is at the end of the coast road to Russell. There is a campsite and parking facilities for cars and trailers. The starting point for the track to Cape Brett and access to Oke Bay runs up beside an old white colonial-style house on the right-hand side of the road going east.

Cape Brett Walk

This is a hard eight to nine hour tramp which starts at Oke Bay. It is mostly across private land and trampers need to contact park headquarters in Russell to arrange permission to cross the land. At Cape Brett accommodation is available in the former lighthouse keeper's quarters, but people need to be totally self-sufficient. There are toilets and fresh water, but no fires are allowed. Take gas or liquid fuel cooking equipment.

Oke Bay

Oke Bay

By land Oke Bay is just a few minutes from Rawhiti, but to get to it by sea it is necessary to go through Albert Channel and around Richards Peninsula.

As you round the peninsula it is hard to see the entrance to the bay and there are a few rocks some distance out from the cliffs. However, if you keep going on a course to avoid the rocks, eventually the entrance will open up. It will be some time before the beach is seen but once into the harbour you will see it is well worth the effort.

Oke Bay is surrounded on three sides by high cliffs. They shelter the anchorage, but a swell rolls into the bay in some easterly conditions. The sandy beach has no real shade and the sun reflecting off the high cliffs can get very hot. However, later in the day, there is some shade from the cliffs as the sun gets further west.

The water can be very clear, which helps to reveal submerged rocks not far off the beach. Beware of these rocks in your dinghy or runabout. If in doubt keep to the left-hand side of the bay.

At the north end of the beach is a steep track up the cliff. At the top you can turn left to the start of the Cape Brett Walk at the power pole, go straight over and down the path to the Rawhiti road, or turn right and visit the graveyard on the hill overlooking Oke Bay. Again there are some wonderful views over the Bay of Islands and out to Cape Brett.

Some people use nearby **Deep Water Cove** as a first stop anchorage after rounding Cape Brett on the trip from the south. However, you do need plenty of anchor chain or warp for safety as it lives up to its name.

Te Puna Inlet

While the islands of the Bay and the coast from Russell to Cape Brett are the most popular cruising areas, the Te Puna Inlet has some bays for those wanting a quieter spot, as well as the Black Rocks and Marsden Cross.

The inlet can be reached either via Kent Passage or by passing round the Black Rocks. When there is a heavy swell from the north or east around the Black Rocks, it is better to use Kent Passage.

If heading for Kent Passage from Opua or the south beware of Brampton Bank. Keep to the Russell side of the green buoy. Remember, green to port going out even where, as here, you are almost enclosed by land.

The passage is very narrow and shallow so keep to the centre. Power lines run across from the mainland to Moturoa Island but there is a clearance of 30 m which should be enough for the average cruising yacht. Once through the passage watch for The Brothers, marked by a beacon, and Slains Castle, unmarked (see Chart 5122 for full details).

There are bays either side of the inlet to suit all weather conditions. However, the bays on the west side do not have proper beaches. It is possible to land but the beaches are shelly mud and not much good for children wanting to play on the sand. If you do not mind the mud you will be rewarded by finding mussels on the rocks and the children can explore the rock pools.

There are no facilities of any kind. The nearest water, fuel and shops are at Kerikeri. Te Puna Inlet is not part of the Bay of Islands Maritime and Historic Park so there are no restrictions on landing with pets other than keeping them off private property.

Black Rocks Scenic Reserve

The Black Rocks are situated off the north and eastern coast of Moturoa Island and formed from basalt lava. The volcano that produced this thick and extensive flow could have been one of several inland cones active more than 1.2 million years ago.

Most of the islets fall sheer to the sea floor. There is very little vegetation but they support many species of birds and are a breeding ground for the black-backed and red-billed gull and the white-fronted tern.

Study your chart well for access to the islets – possible in very calm conditions. There is some excellent diving and fishing. However, more often than not there is a swell around the rocks.

Marsden Cross Historic Reserve

A simple cross of Celtic pattern stands on the shore at Oihi in Rangihoua Bay at the end of Purerua Peninsula and marks the spot where the Rev. Samuel Marsden preached his first sermon in New Zealand on Christmas Day 1814. Marsden was invited to New Zealand by the chief Ruatara. Marsden had nursed him on a voyage from London to Sydney and Ruatara acted as interpreter for the first sermon.

The cross also marks the site of the Church Missionary Society's first mission station and the birthplace of the first recorded European child to be born in New Zealand – Thomas King, born on 20 February 1815 to John King, one of the pioneer missionaries, and his wife.

The Marsden Cross Historic Reserve is part of the Bay of Islands Maritime and Historic Park. It can be reached by land as well as by sea. Road access is through Mataka Station, which is privately owned. The entrance is well signposted beneath the farm manager's house on Rangihoua Road (reached from Kerikeri via Landing Road, Kapiro Road and Purerua Road or from SH10 via Waipapa to Kapiro Road and Purerua Road). It is an easy walk of about 40 minutes each way and visitors are asked to observe the landowner's conditions of entry displayed at the start of the walk. The bay is suitable for swimming and a picnic.

The East Coast

from the Bay of Islands to Whangarei

The coast between the Bay of Islands and Whangarei contains several bays suitable for anchorage if you do not want to cover the distance in one trip. And for those with energy to be active, the area offers many attractions.

The waters around the Poor Knights Islands provide a delightful playground for divers, as described in Appendix II. The whole area is popular with anglers looking for large game fish. Those wishing to stay on or close to the shore can enjoy pleasant swimming beaches and scenic walks with panoramic views.

Whangarei itself is a popular boating stop, with a full range of facilities as well as a wide variety of recreational pursuits. A word of warning: travel with the tide up the long harbour entrance to the Town Basin!

Tutukaka

Facilities

 FUEL   in marina.

 GAS BOTTLES   at dive shop.

 WATER   in marina.

 STORES   dairy and take-aways.

 HARBOUR-MASTER   office in marina, telephone NG (089-33) 441.

 TELEPHONE   near the shops.

 REPAIRS   slipway with all marine repairs and chandlery.

 DIVE AIR   at dive shop.

 EATING OUT   hotel with restaurant.

 FISHING   Deep Sea Anglers Club welcomes visitors.

 TRANSPORT   bus service to Whangarei.

 ACCOMMODATION   tourist resort and motel.

Tutukaka Harbour marina

Tutukaka is a resort not far up the coast from Whangarei Harbour and is popular with divers and deep sea anglers. The Poor Knights Islands, which provide some magnificent diving, are just a short distance off the coast and the nearby waters provide excellent opportunities for game fishing.

It is a safe harbour in all but strong easterlies and there is a marina, administered by the Northland Harbour Board, with visitors' berths and all facilities. The berth charge includes the use of power, water, showers, etc.

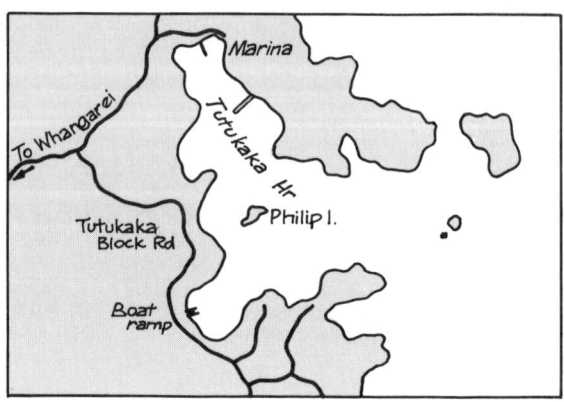

Anchorage

As well as the marina berths, there is room for boats to anchor, with landing for dinghies, on several beaches around the harbour. The land is not part of any maritime park.

Launching ramp

Concrete to low water with good parking.

Mimiwhangata

Mimiwhangata is on the headland outside the entrance to Whangaruru Harbour, a little over half-way between Bream Head and Cape Brett. It is a farm and marine park, established to preserve the many forms of life in the coastal waters and administered by the Bay of Islands Maritime and Historic Park.

There are two bays, Mimiwhangata Beach and Okupe Beach, the first being the more sheltered. Both are sandy with good swimming. The only facilities are toilets and water. Visitors arriving by road must leave their vehicles in the car-park.

There are several walks in the reserve. A two-hour loop walk around the headland combines a little of everything – coastal scenery, archaeological sites, sandy beaches, rocky shores, farmland and native vegetation. Please keep to the paths when crossing sand dunes so the ground-nesting birds are not disturbed.

Because it is a reserve there are some restrictions. No camping or visitors after dark, no domestic pets, no fires and no vehicles in the park. Line anglers

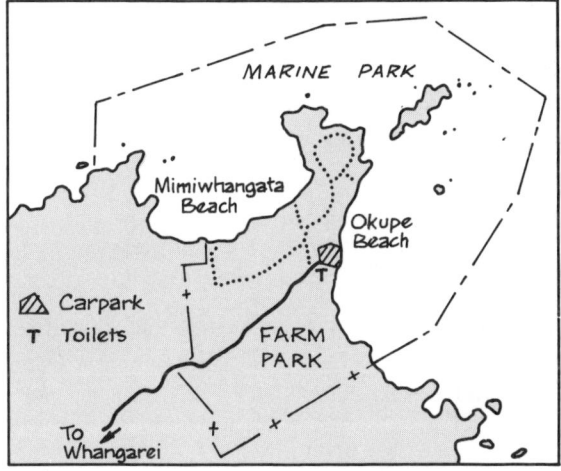

may use only unweighted single-hooked lines and are limited, as are spear fishermen, to taking pelagic fish species only – that is, species of the open sea. No nets or longlines allowed.

Whangaruru

Facilities (Oakura)

 FUEL at store.

 GAS BOTTLES at store.

 STORES groceries, wine and postage
 facilities.

 SHOWERS/LAUNDRY washing machines
and driers for hire at motor camp.

 DIVE AIR at motor camp.

 POOLS Hot pool, cold pool, spa pool for
hire at motor camp.

 BOATS for hire at motor camp.

 TRACTOR for hire at motor camp if you
want to launch a boat.

 ACCOMMODATION motels, cabins and
camp sites with power at motor camp. If you
are meeting friends and want to leave your
car somewhere safe, check with the motor
camp. Parking is allowed when possible.

Whangaruru, meaning sheltered harbour, lives up to its name. It is a good place to spend a day or two on the way up the coast. There are several beaches and the harbour itself provides various recreational opportunities, such as dinghy sailing, diving and excellent fishing.

To port going up the harbour is **Oakura**, a seaside resort with accommodation and stores. It has good road access and a launching ramp for runabouts. The beach is long and sandy and boats can also be launched off the beach. It is not a reserve so there is no restriction on landing.

Whangaruru North Head

On the opposite side of the harbour is Whangaruru North Head which is part of the Bay of Islands Maritime and Historic Park. One side is in the harbour and the other on the open sea. The harbour side has several sandy beaches for swimming and picnics, and a campsite at Puriri Bay.

Road access to Whangaruru North Head is via Ngaiotonga off the Whangarei–Russell Road. There are toilets and fresh water and open-air showers, but campers should take their own cooking equipment (gas or liquid fuel). On arrival campers should report to the farm manager or ranger. No reservations are taken and the maximum stay during the peak summer period is three weeks. The camp is closed between 1 July and 30 September each year. No domestic animals are allowed in the reserve.

There are several walks around the headland. Most start at Puriri Bay. The walk to Rangiaukaha Trig provides panoramic views of the surrounding harbour and coastline.

Pohutukawa fringe the rocky coastal areas of the reserve. Known as the New Zealand Christmas tree, the pohutukawa's red flowers come out in December and are a magnificent sight in full bloom. Puriri and

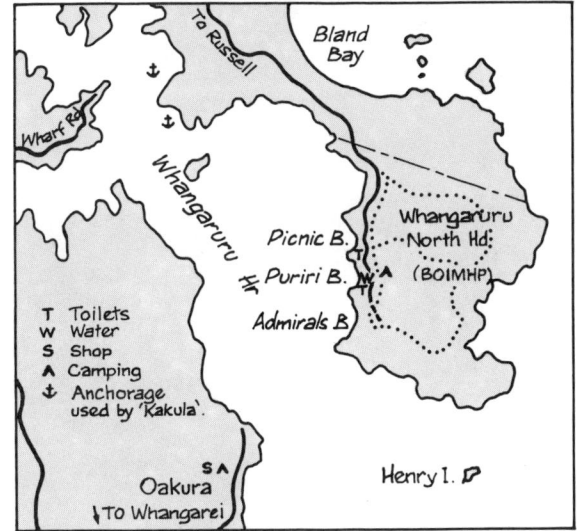

kowhai flourish in the bush and rare species of fern, orchid, native fuchsia and convolvulus are to be found. The bush is also refuge to a rare species of land snail. Birds which inhabit the area include the kiwi, fantail, welcome swallow, tui, kingfisher, oystercatcher, heron, gannet and white-fronted tern.

Other anchorages

There are other anchorages further up the harbour with landing for dinghies on beaches. Passing to port of Motukauri and proceeding up the harbour there is a headland with moorings at the end. There is road access to the few houses at this point and a walk along the road provides views out over the harbour. This is not reserve land so you can take your dog for a walk.

Whangamumu

Whangamumu Harbour is accessible only by boat or on foot along the track which runs from the Rawhiti road. Today it is a quiet reserve, part of the Bay of Islands Maritime and Historic Park, but during the whaling days it was a hive of activity.

It can be tricky finding the entrance to the harbour from the south, particularly in bad weather when white water everywhere can be a bit daunting. However, once inside it is sheltered, apart from a swell in easterly conditions.

As you enter the harbour the site of the old whaling station is to starboard and at the end of the harbour is a beach and camping area. There are no facilities at the camp ground other than water.

Old whaling machinery, Whangamumu

Whangamumu Harbour

Campers should be self-sufficient in all other respects. No domestic animals allowed.

The original whaling station was built in 1844, but it was not until 1892, when an easier method of catching the whales was developed, that Whangamumu became famous. By 1899 about 20 local men were employed and the station prospered until the early 1930s. The largest recorded catch was 74 humpback whales in 1927. Today the whale is protected in New Zealand waters.

Pictorial and written signs on a rock cairn at the whaling station site and the remains of vats, a boiler and two concrete slipways give some insight into whaling life.

Whangarei

Chart No: 521 Cape Brett to Bream Tail
Chart No: 5213 Approaches to Marsden Point: Whangarei Harbour
Map No: Infomap I N20/24

Facilities

 FUEL Orams Marine on starboard side of river just before the Town Basin or, in cans, from garage on corner of John Street and Robert Street.

 GAS BOTTLES refilled at Caltex garage at end of Walton Street, under railway bridge and into Tarewa Road. The best value gas in the North!

 KEROSENE garage on corner of John Street and Robert Street.

 WATER several taps on the river bank and wharf but need a long hose to reach the boat if filling up while on a pile mooring. We filled bottles and poured the water from them into the tanks.

  STORES Whangarei has every store imaginable so you can buy what you want if you can find it. For daily requirements such as bread and milk there are two dairies across the road from the Basin in Riverside Drive. There is also a take-away bar.

A few stores particularly relevant to boaties' needs are:
Pak 'N' Save – a grocery store for those on a budget, just along the road from the Basin in Walton Street. If you want to stock up the boat with more than you can carry, Pak 'N' Save allow their trundlers to be taken down to the Basin on payment of a $10 deposit at the checkout control desk. This is refunded when you return the trundler.

Arthur's Emporium – a wonderland of bargains, some of them useful, such as netting, tape, tools, fabric and sewing items, household utensils, gifts. A fun place to look around.
Chandlery – there are several chandlery stores on both sides of the river. If you need something you may want to shop around for the best price. Some of the boatyards have a store and will give people using the yard a better price on their purchases.
Banks – there are branches of all major banks and building societies scattered around the main shopping centre.

 RUBBISH DISPOSAL bins on river bank emptied daily.

  TOILETS/SHOWERS separate facilities for men and women in the building in front of the swimming pool beside the Olympic dairy and on the other side of the river in the Harbour Board building opposite the plywood store. The key which fits all the doors is available from the Harbour Board office when you pay for your berth. There is a deposit of $10 on the key and the showers are operated by putting a coin in the meter – 50 cents for the showers in front of the pool and 20 cents for the others (due to be increased to 50 cents).

 LAUNDRY washing machine and two large tubs with hot water. Washing machine takes 50 cent coins, no charge for using the tubs.

No drying facilities. One key gives access to the laundry and shower blocks.

 HARBOUR-MASTER Ron Knox, telephone 487-099

 TELEPHONE outside Olympic Swimming Pool or at post office.

 FIRST AID look in the Yellow Pages for full listing of doctors, dentists, etc. Whangarei

Veterinary Service will make boat calls to overseas yachts which cannot land their animals for quarantine reasons.

 POSTAL Rathbone Street. All facilities, including banking, holding mail, postal and telephones.

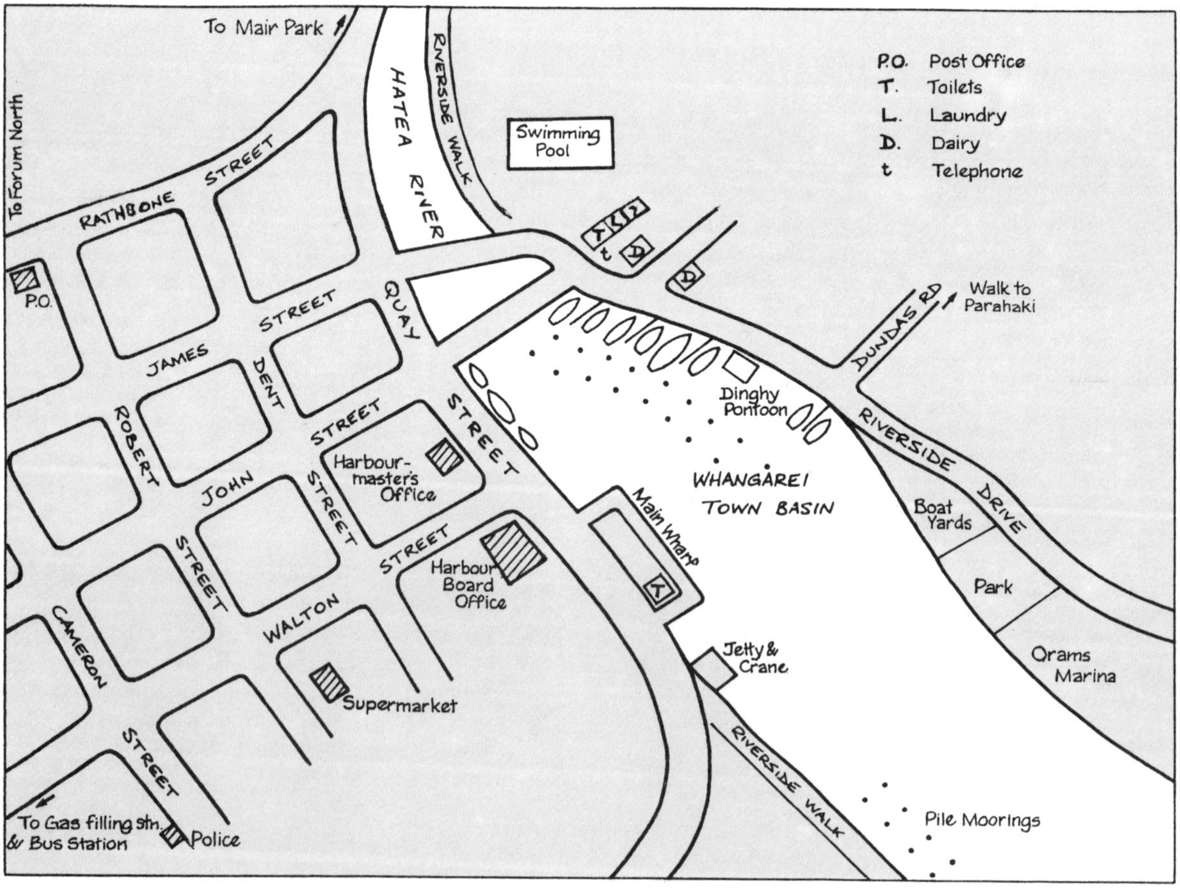

Captain Cook and members of his crew were the earliest Europeans to see the area now called Whangarei. Cook left a permanent record of his visit by naming Bream Head. His diary records that no sooner had the ship anchored than the crew caught between 90 and 100 bream, thus the name.

Whangarei is one of the earliest settlements in New Zealand, although the name originally applied to a small place near the heads. Traders bartering with the Maori found Ahipupu, now the Town Basin area, a more satisfactory point for meeting, as it is today.

Newcomers to Whangarei are sometimes surprised to find that the city itself, although an official Port of Entry to New Zealand, is so far inland. The distance from the heads to the Town Basin is 15 miles and should be travelled with the tide as there is quite a strong current.

Whangarei has all facilities for boaties either for replenishing supplies, repairs or recreation. The Northland Harbour Board administers the Town Basin and provides pile berths and jetties for visitors. There are toilets, showers and laundry alongside the Basin.

It is very popular with overseas boats during the cyclone season, but it also provides a stopping-off point for boats on a cruise along the east coast. There is plenty for all ages in Whangarei and if your crew has been in the islands with nothing but sea and sand they might appreciate a change.

If you arrive off the Heads too late to make the Town Basin by nightfall, or at the wrong stage of the tide, there are two bays on the starboard side of the harbour which provide overnight anchorages.

Urquharts Bay

Entry to any of the bays in Whangarei Harbour requires a good study of the appropriate chart. There are many shallow areas which dry at low tide. The anchorage in Urquharts will be obvious from the permanent moorings, but watch for a deep hole (marked on the chart) as you will wonder where all your anchor warp is going if you drop anchor at that point.

Urquharts Bay has a few houses but no facilities for boaties. It is on the road from Whangarei which turns sharply over the peninsula to Ocean Beach after reaching Urquharts Bay. There is a pleasant walk over Bream Head to Smuggler's Cove. No dogs allowed on the walk but they can land on the beach.

The beach is shelly and shallow with easy landing for dinghies although the tide goes out quite a way and you will have to pull the dinghy well up the beach. There is a launching ramp, concrete to half tide, but not much room for parking.

McLeods Bay

This is the next bay on the starboard side of the harbour suitable for an overnight anchorage. It lies in the lee of Mount Manaia which provides shelter, but at times the wind can come round either side of the mountain causing rough conditions in the bay. There are some permanent moorings and a small wharf used by commercial fishermen.

McLeods Bay is a residential area with houses along the beachfront. It has a few shops at a little shopping centre up the road to the right of the beach. There is also a telephone box. There is no water or fuel, or other facilities.

The beach is shelly and shallow with the tide going a long way out at low tide. The main road to Whangarei runs beside the beach and there is a commuters' bus service to the city morning and evening.

Many of the locals are of Scottish descent. When the Scots were forced by the Highland Clearances to leave their land many went to Nova Scotia but finding the climate too harsh moved on to Australia and New Zealand. Some of these migrants settled in the Whangarei Heads area. The Presbyterian Church in McLeods Bay was built two or three years after the first settlers arrived in 1858.

Anchorage

There is no recognised anchorage beyond Parua Bay as it is all part of the main channel to Whangarei. However, an emergency shelter can be found near Limestone Island. The Northland Harbour Board provides some pile berths and jetties in the Town Basin and at Kissing Point further out from the city. There are also visitors' berths available at Orams Marine just before the Town Basin, telephone 488-521. Pleasure craft are not allowed to use the berths at Port Whangarei, which is for commercial shipping only.

To arrange a berth in the Town Basin tie up beside the main wharf and go to the harbour-master's office. The Harbour Board occupies a large office block on the corner of Walton Street and Quay Street on the left-hand side of the basin. The

Whangarei Harbour

Harbour-master is in the cream single-storey building on the opposite corner of Walton Street.

Overseas yachts will already have called ahead to arrange clearance and for them there is a $50 port entry fee.

Berth fees depend on the type of berth you take. The convenience of being able to step ashore will cost more, but if you have children or are staying for some time it could be worth it. On the other hand if you do not mind a short row each time you go ashore a pile berth is cheaper. Landing is no problem as there are jetties at regular intervals along the waterfront and ladders allow access at all stages of the tide — except for the less agile.

Launching ramps

There is no launching ramp in the Town Basin but there are plenty scattered around Whangarei Harbour:

Limeburners Creek – concrete, fair parking.

Marsden Bay – concrete from Domain area to below high water, good parking.

Marsden Point – concrete to half tide, good parking.

One Tree Point – concrete to low water, fair parking.

Oakleigh – concrete to low water, fair parking.

Onerahi – concrete to low water, good parking.

Onerahi Road – concrete to below half tide, owned by Onerahi Cruising Club.

Onerahi Yacht Club – concrete, owned by Club.

Parua Bay – concrete to low water, excellent parking.

Stephens Point – concrete, constructed and owned by Sea Scouts.

Waikaraka – concrete to below half tide, owned by Outboard Boating Club.

Tamaterau – metal, giving access to beach, fair parking.

Tamaterau–Browns Bay – concrete, giving access to beach, poor parking.

Reotahi – concrete, small, giving access to beach, poor parking.

Urquharts Bay – concrete to half tide, poor parking.

Recreation

Forum North

For information on what is on in Whangarei while you are there go to Forum North in Rust Avenue. This is the cultural centre of Northland containing a theatre, exhibition hall, activity rooms, restaurant and bar, and the public relations office.

Clapham Clock Museum

This is a fascinating place for all ages. It has about a thousand clocks and watches, many of them novelty items. The collection was started by Mr Archie Clapham and donated to the Whangarei City Council. Mr Clapham had a great sense of humour and there are some clocks in the collection which he made himself. There are also antique clocks.

The museum is open from 10 a.m. to 4 p.m. weekdays and 10.15 a.m. to 3 p.m. on weekends. It is a popular stop with tour buses passing through Whangarei, so if you visit at the same time as a tour party you can tag along for the conducted tour.

Art Gallery

Through the city library is the North Gallery, a small art gallery featuring monthly exhibitions of works by New Zealand artists and craftspeople. The gallery is administered by the Northland Society of Arts which also runs Reyburn House near the Town Basin. The North Gallery is open from 10.30 a.m. to 4.30 p.m. weekdays only.

Reyburn House

Reyburn House, beside the river at the end of Quay Street, is an old colonial house which has been converted into an art gallery. Opening times depend on the volunteers who run it so telephone 483-074 to check.

City Library

Next to Forum North is the City Library. Visitors are able to borrow books on a visitor's ticket which costs $2. There is no charge for reading books in the library and there is also a good selection of newspapers and magazines. If you require

Town Basin moorings, Whangarei

information about Northland this will probably be found in the Northland Room, but these books may not be taken away from the library. The library is open Monday to Thursday 9 a.m. to 7 p.m., Friday 9 a.m. to 8 p.m. and Saturday 10 a.m. to noon.

Swimming pools

There are both indoor and outdoor pools in the Ted Eliot Memorial complex opposite the Town Basin. The indoor pool is heated and has a spa and sauna. The outdoor pool is Olympic size and has a diving pool, children's and toddlers' pools and a water slide.

Opening times vary depending on the time of year but are given on a board outside.

Cinemas

There are two cinemas in Whangarei, the Odeon in Cameron Street and the Regent in Bank Street.

Parahaki Scenic Reserve

Bush-clad Parahaki dominates the eastern approaches to Whangarei and has outstanding views from its summit. At night you can see the light on the war memorial. There are three clearly marked walks up Parahaki. Two leave from Mair Park and the other from Dundas Road. All converge on the summit.

If you start at Dundas Road (the road alongside the Portobello Motor Inn on Riverside Drive), there is a waterfall a short way up this track which makes a good turning point for a short walk. Otherwise carry on up the path through the native bush which includes kauri, totara, kahikatea, rimu, miro and matai. The view from the top will make it worth the effort.

Go down by the Drummond Track which starts behind the building at the summit. There is a track near the steps and the Drummond Track is the left-hand fork at the junction. This will bring you down into Mair Park which is ideal for a picnic beside the river. The walk back to the Town Basin is along Hatea Drive. The round trip takes about two and a half hours, but allow extra for a picnic. While it is steep in parts it is not too difficult for those of average fitness. It can, however, be slippery after rain.

Youth centre

At the time of writing the local police were running a youth centre in John Street called the Blue Light Centre. Activities include roller-skating.

Bowling centre

A tenpin bowling centre is near the Town Basin in Dent Street.

Children's playgrounds

On the Parahaki walk you will notice the playground in Mair Park at the Rurumoki Street entrance.

There is also a children's playground closer to the Town Basin in Riverside Drive next door to Orams Marina.

Parua Bay

When you have had enough of the city, replenished your supplies and want to get your sea-legs back, a good first stop is Parua Bay on the way down the harbour towards the open sea.

Study your chart well to find the entrance to the Bay. A popular anchorage is the Nook which is sheltered from most winds. The channel into the Bay passes to starboard of the beacon off the Nook.

Further into the Bay is the Parua Bay Tavern on the water's edge. It is one of the few waterside pubs in New Zealand and boaties are encouraged to tie up at the wharf and go ashore. In summer there is a barbecue available. You pay a set price for a salad and piece of meat, then cook your meat to your own liking on the barbecue. There are tables on the lawn.

The Hauraki Gulf area

The Hauraki Gulf Maritime Park, New Zealand's first maritime park, was established in 1967 to protect 47 islands in order to retain the unspoiled and often rare vegetation, provide a haven for animal and bird life and, equally important, provide recreation and enjoyment for the public.

The islands can be divided into two types — recreation or inner islands and conservation or outer islands. The recreational islands are those, such as Motutapu, Rangitoto and Motuihe, which are close to Auckland and used regularly by the public.

Conservation islands are more difficult to get to and have few natural beaches so they are being used to provide sanctuaries for the preservation of native species of plants and animals. Landing by the public is prohibited. These are:

Little Barrier Island (people with a genuine interest in the wildlife of the island may be given a permit to land)
Aldermen Islands
Bream Islands
Cuvier Island
Hen and Chicken Islands
Mercury Islands (except Great Mercury, which is privately owned)
Mokohinau Islands (except Burgess)
Poor Knights Islands (diving allowed around the coast)
Sail Rock

Some islands of the gulf have areas belonging to the park with the remainder being privately owned. These include Great Barrier Island.

Auckland

Chart No: 532 Approaches to Auckland
Chart No: 5321 Kawau Island to Rangitoto Island
Chart No: 5322 Auckland Harbour
Chart No: 5324 Tamaki Strait and Approaches including Waiheke Island

Map No: Infomap 262 Sheet 3 for overview of Auckland and Gulf Infomap 260 R11 for more detail of Auckland

Facilities at Westhaven Marina

 FUEL Orams Marine 8 a.m. to 5 p.m. seven days. Royal New Zealand Yacht Squadron 9 a.m. to 1 p.m. Tuesday, Wednesday and Thursday; 9 a.m. to 5 p.m. Friday, Saturday and Sunday.

 GAS/KEROSENE gas at Auckland Gas Company and kerosene at Caltex garage – see map.

 WATER there are several taps along each jetty.

 STORES all the shops around Westhaven are marine related services such as sail makers, chandlers, electricians and riggers. There are two lunch bars which sell a few basic items such as bread and milk but no other stores. For groceries you will have to go either to the mini-market in the Downtown Shopping Centre, Victoria Street Market or Ponsonby. See map for directions.

 BANKS there are branches of all major banks in Auckland and also offices of Thomas Cook and American Express for overseas visitors.

 RUBBISH DISPOSAL jumbo rubbish bins emptied daily.

 SHOWERS/TOILETS there are public toilets open 24 hours and showers accessible only by key available from the Marina Supervisor on payment of a $10 deposit. The marina charge includes showers.

 LAUNDRY none and washing is not supposed to be hung out in the marina. There are laundry facilities in Ponsonby.

 TELEPHONE public telephone boxes in the marina.

 POLICE Wharf Police Office on Quay Street just along from Queen Elizabeth Square and CPO; Ph: 794-500. Main police station in Vincent Street; Ph: 794-240.

 FIRST AID Accident and Emergency at Auckand Hospital. Doctors listed in telephone book.

REPAIRS   several grids in the marina for launches and yachts. Free but on a first-come-first-served basis and naturally in most demand at weekends. The free grids are available for two tides for hull cleaning and quick repairs. There are long-stay grids which can be booked and there is a charge. Auckland Harbour Board provides haul-out facilities at Okahu Bay, a few kilometres along the waterfront, for boats up to 10 tonnes. There are several private travelift companies in Westhaven.

 POWER   power points on the jetties, some are 110 volts but transformers available for hire if necessary from the electrician in the marina.

 POSTAL   Auckland Central Post Office is opposite the Downtown Shopping Centre, about 20 minutes' walk from Westhaven.

 EATING OUT   there is a restaurant in the marina but it is very upmarket – the Porches and Mercedes outside will prove this. If you want to dine in style (with the corresponding expense) it is a very nice restaurant but is not the place to go if you have spent all day cleaning the boat on the grid and want a quick meal while you wait for the tide to float her off! In Auckland itself there are dozens of restaurants, cafes and fast food outlets for all tastes and budgets. In Victoria Park Market there are stalls selling all kinds of ethnic food. Tables and chairs are provided in the courtyard where you can eat your choice of food.

 TRANSPORT   within walking distance of Westhaven are the railway and bus stations and the Downtown Airline Terminal which has a regular shuttle bus service to Auckland International Airport. For sightseeing around Auckland the local bus company, the Auckland Regional Authority, offers discount fares. There is an information kiosk at the bus station.

 LOCAL RADIO   1ZB 1080, 1ZM 1251 and several private stations give local news and weather regularly through the day.

 WEATHER FORECAST   telephone 799-611 or VHF Channel 21.

Auckand is the largest city in New Zealand and is known as the City of Sails because so many boats and boating events are based there. It is an official Port of Entry for overseas boats.

The city is on an isthmus between the Manukau Harbour on the west coast and the Waitemata Harbour on the east coast. The west coast does not have much to offer the recreational boatie other than fishing. The Tasman Sea is rough and there is a bar at the harbour mouth.

However, the Waitemata Harbour on the east coast runs into the Hauraki Gulf and there are several islands and beaches for recreation, some within an hour of Auckland.

Visitors from overseas in their own boats will find all the facilities they need for repairs and provisioning at Westhaven Marina at the end of the harbour beneath the harbour bridge. It is administered by the Auckland Harbour Board.

Charterers will probably pick up their boats at Westhaven or Half Moon Bay Marina which is a little way up the Tamaki River in the city's eastern suburbs.

Most of the islands in the Gulf belong to the Hauraki Gulf Maritime Park and are protected on behalf of the people of New Zealand. There are 47 islands in the park and one mainland reserve. Together they have important wildlife, conservation, scientific and historic value, and offer a wide range of recreational opportunities.

Waiheke Island and Great Barrier Island are more residential and only small parts of these islands are part of the park. In fact, Waiheke is almost a suburb of Auckland with many workers commuting to the city to work each day.

The Auckland harbours and the Hauraki Gulf do not have the problems of sudden wind gusts peculiar to the Marlborough Sounds. However, sea breezes

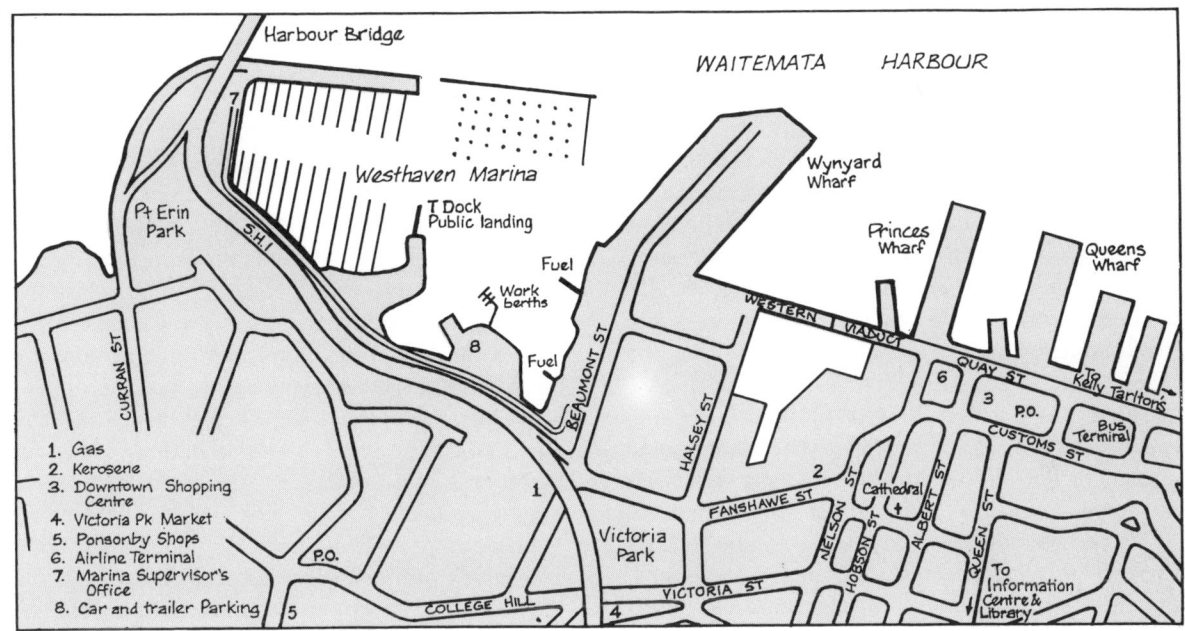

1. Gas
2. Kerosene
3. Downtown Shopping Centre
4. Victoria Pk Market
5. Ponsonby Shops
6. Airline Terminal
7. Marina Supervisor's Office
8. Car and trailer Parking

come up in the afternoon so be aware that a day trip which starts out on a calm morning may turn into something a bit stronger for the return home. The Coast Guard provides a 24-hour weather forecast on VHF Channel 21 which will give you some idea of what to expect.

If you are visiting Auckland on a holiday cruise in order to reprovision be prepared for a bit of a walk. There are no general food stores near Westhaven marina, just lunch bars which stock a few items such as milk and bread. There is a supermarket in the Downtown Shopping Centre at the bottom of Queen Street and more shops in Ponsonby, a suburb just out of the city centre. There are also some food stores in the Victoria Street Market not far from Westhaven.

Chandlery and marine services are much handier. Most marine services are located around the perimeter of Westhaven.

Auckland has so many attractions that visitors with only a few days in the city will find it hard to decide which to choose. Children will enjoy the zoo, the Museum of Transport and Technology and Kelly Tarlton's Underwater World – all readily accessible by bus or on foot

For adults there are art galleries, shops, library, theatres and cinemas, historic buildings and the Auckland Institute and Museum. The Polynesian section of the museum will be of particular interest to overseas boaties who have sailed through the Pacific, and the Maori hall is also interesting.

Many people using this book will live in Auckland with their own mooring or berth and will find the following information irrelevant. However, overseas visitors and those visiting Auckland from other parts of the country can waste many hours looking for the services and facilities they require, so the following information is for them.

Westhaven Marina

This is the largest of New Zealand's marinas with 1200 marina berths, 276 pile moorings and 85 swing moorings. It is administered by the Auckland Harbour Board and approximately 30 of the berths or piles scattered throughout the marina are available for visitors, the largest suitable for a 20 m craft.

It is about 20 minutes' walk from the heart of Auckland city. It can be noisy as it is right under the harbour bridge and the approach roads run beside the marina. However, this has to be offset against the convenience of being close to the amenities a big city offers. The marina is well lit at night and patrolled by a security guard.

Approaching from the sea you will probably come into the harbour through the Rangitoto Channel – that is, between the mainland and the famous conical-shaped island Rangitoto. Turn to starboard around North Head and make your way towards the harbour bridge. Westhaven is to port just before the bridge. There are two entrances in the breakwater. It does not matter which you take, although one is wider. Be warned that if you come in early on a weekend morning you will be going against the flow of weekend sailors taking their boats out for the racing on the harbour.

To book a visitor's berth write to the Marina Supervisor, Westhaven, Auckland Harbour Board, Private Bag, Auckland, or telephone Auckland (09) 391-352. Charges vary so check at time of booking. The marina becomes very busy in summer and it is best to book as far ahead as possible. Out-of-Auckland boats may stay for a maximum of three months.

If you do arrive without a booking, tie up to 'T' dock, which is for short-term docking, and go to the Marina Supervisor's office, close to the Sitting Duck lunch bar beside the harbour bridge piles. 'T' dock is not for long-term stays; the signs on the wharf say one hour is allowed and it is regularly patrolled to enforce this limit.

The pole moorings are difficult to use because of the strong tidal current flowing through the breakwater. Privately owned piles have permanent ropes attached which can be picked up with the boat-hook. However, on those that do not have this facility it is best to berth at slack water or take the dinghy and attach ropes first.

Some of the jetties have high gates at the shore end which are locked at night. If you are on one of these jetties and expect to be out late, you will have to leave your dinghy somewhere so you can row back to your boat.

It is also possible for larger vessels to use space

Westhaven, Auckland

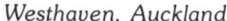

Anniversary Day, Auckland Harbour

15 m but living aboard is not allowed. However, overseas visitors are allowed to live on boats on the hardstand area while carrying out repairs. A travelift is available for haul-outs and a full range of on-site services include engineers, boat builders and a spar loft. There are toilets and showers. Bookings for berths to Half Moon Bay Marina, PO Box 54-021, Bucklands Beach, Auckland; telephone (09) 534-3139.

For cruisers calling in for supplies, there are large shopping centres nearby at Highland Park, Pakuranga and Howick which can be reached by taxi.

at Marsden Wharf, among the commercial shipping wharves. Bookings for this should be made by contacting the Harbour-master, Auckland Harbour Board, Private Bag, Auckland. Telephone (09) 795-950.

While living aboard a boat is not technically allowed, obviously overseas visitors have to live on their boats if they have no shore accommodation. There are usually several boats in Westhaven with people living on board and, whatever the authorities might think, they provide a bit of colour and interest for the thousands of people who wander around the marina just for a look. Locals like to talk to visitors, ask them about their voyage to New Zealand and sometimes even invite them home, or offer help with transport or repairs.

Half Moon Bay Marina

Half Moon Bay Marina is up the Tamaki River in Auckland's eastern suburbs. Fuel, a full range of repair services and a small shopping centre, including groceries, chandlery and dive shop, are available. It is also a yacht charter base.

The marina is surrounded by high quality homes and is close to the popular sandy beaches at Eastern Beach and Bucklands Beach. The river itself is very busy at weekends with boats from the marina and other moorings going out into the gulf and dinghies and sailboards skimming the water.

Marina berths are available for visiting craft up to

Launching ramps

There are many launching ramps in Auckland and the Auckland Harbour Board administers two, at Westhaven Marina and Okahu Bay. Both have ample parking for cars and trailers. A launch/park permit is required and is available from the marina or Okahu Bay. This should be displayed while you are parked in the car-park. Trailer and boat storage is also available in both areas.

Other ramps are located along the waterfront at Mission Bay, Kohimarama and St Heliers, in the eastern suburbs at Bucklands Beach, Cockle Bay, Howick, Beachlands and Maraetai, and along the North Shore at Bayswater, Birkenhead, Browns Bay, Castor Bay, Devonport, Mairangi Bay, Milford, Murrays Bay, Northcote, Rothesay Bay, Takapuna and Torbay.

Recreation

Because opening times and admission prices of recreation venues change we will just give a general description of suitable activities for a few hours' shore leave, keeping in mind visiting boaties are not likely to have a vehicle. For fuller details visit the tourist information centre in Aotea Square, half-way up Queen Street (the main street) on the right-hand side from the waterfront and just before the Town Hall. Besides information on all the local attractions, there are maps of the city and copies of the local tourist newspaper giving details of events.

Victoria Park Market

Walk to the end of the marina and out to the main road. You will be looking at a sports field and across the other side is a big brick chimney. This is Victoria Park Market. Open seven days a week, it is full of stalls selling all kinds of clothes, jewellery, crafts, foodstuffs, books – in fact, you name it, they probably sell it. Even if you are not buying, it is interesting to walk around just people-watching. There is a very good vegetable store which also sells herbs. There is also a bakery for fresh crusty bread, a butcher, a fishmonger, health food store, an ice-cream parlour as well as a variety of ready-to-eat food.

The adjacent Victoria Park is a good spot for the children to kick a ball around and has a children's playground with swings, slides, etc.

Museum of Transport and Technology

This museum, known to the locals as MOTAT, is in Great North Road, Western Springs. It is a short journey by regular bus service from Downtown Auckand. The museum contains many old vehicles, trains, trams and machinery. Old houses have been furnished in the colonial style and some old shops stocked with the things they sold in their heyday. It is open every day.

Auckland Zoological Park

Just around the corner from MOTAT is the Auckland Zoo. Of particular interest to overseas visitors is the Kiwi House. Because the birds are nocturnal the Kiwi House is darkened, but you soon get used to the gloom. The zoo has the usual range of animals and birds in pleasantly laid out grounds, and there is a coffee bar for refreshment.

Kelly Tarlton's Underwater World

For boaties who do not dive and particularly children, this is the place to see what is under the water you sail over! Instead of humans looking at animals in cages as at the zoo, fish and mammals swim around in their natural element, while the humans are confined to a perspex tunnel.

The centre was set up by one of New Zealand's best known divers, Kelly Tarlton. Unfortunately Kelly died soon after Underwater World was completed. It is situated along the waterfront just past Okahu

Victoria Park Market

Bay, not too far out of town. You could walk there if you are energetic, but it would be too far for children. However, buses leave regularly from the bus station for the drive along the waterfront and on weekends and holidays there is a free Fun Bus. There is a coffee bar for refreshment.

Okahu Bay, opposite the centre, is one of the swimming beaches closest to the city so you could take your togs (swimming costume/bathers) and make a day of it. There is a big park opposite the beach, with swings for the children and public toilets beside the beach.

Closer to the city along the waterfront are a mini-golf course, bumper boats and a swimming-pool with water slide.

North Head

For a busman's holiday take a ferry trip across the harbour to Devonport and walk to North Head, the high point at the end of the Devonport peninsula. Catch the Devonport ferry from the ferry building opposite Queen Elizabeth Square at the bottom of Queen Street. On arrival at Devonport walk along the waterfront road to the right, past the Devonport Yacht Club and around the corner at the end where you can see a sign on a side road leading to North Head, opposite the sports field.

North Head is part of the Hauraki Gulf Maritime Park. It is an old volcano providing an ideal site for the defence of the harbour and was once known as Fort Cautley, an important base for army operations in the north.

Guns were installed on the headland in 1885 during the Russian scare when an invasion by the Russian Pacific fleet was rumoured. The largest gun was a 14-ton eight-inch breech-loading disappearing gun shipped from England. The concrete on which it was mounted had to be cured for a year before the gun could be fired and a new wharf and gantry had to be built to manoeuvre the gun into position. Two more guns were added in 1887.

Further guns were installed and manned during the First World War.

In 1959 Fort Cautley was transferred to Narrow Neck, another North Shore suburb not far from Devonport, but one disappearing gun and four 18-pound field guns remain for the public to inspect. Occasionally the Park Board arranges guided tours of the tunnels. If you want a look be sure to take a torch.

These days North Head has more peaceful uses. It provides a magnificent view of the Gulf and is one of the vantage points from which spectators watch yacht races, such as the Whitbread Round the World race.

Mt Victoria to North Head, Devonport

Auckland Public Library

A good spot for a rainy day – and not so far as the museum – is the Auckland Public Library. It has a good selection of books, magazines, newspapers and reference material. There is also a rare book room and a children's section. There are plenty of comfy chairs to sit in while you read. During school holidays there are special activity programmes for children so if you have youngsters on board check at the information desk.

To get to the library, walk up Queen Street to Wellesley Street East, not quite as far as the information centre on the opposite side of the road. The library entrance is in the first road on the right off Wellesley Street East.

Auckland Institute and Museum

This is a great place for a rainy day and everyone will find something of interest. It is open daily, admission free.

We particularly enjoy the Polynesian section which has many examples of Polynesian craft and information about the early voyagers. For the nautically minded there is a section on maritime history with models of old ships and memorabilia. Children may enjoy the natural history and military sections.

Overseas visitors find the Maori hall fascinating. It has replicas of a Maori meeting house, food storage hut, and a magnificent example of a war canoe. Glass cases around the hall display kiwi feather cloaks, greenstone items and many other artefacts of the early Maori.

The museum is in the Auckland Domain, which is ideal for a good walk or a picnic. There is plenty of space for children to run around and a magnificent view over the harbour.

Get to the Domain by taking the Parnell bus from the bus station and getting off opposite the building of the Royal Foundation for the Blind. Cross the road – there is a pedestrian crossing – and turn down any of the roads on that side. They all lead towards the Domain and you will see the imposing building of the museum on the hill.

Alternatively, the Domain can be reached through the gates beside Auckland Hospital. Walk up Symonds Street, past some of the university buildings, as far as Grafton Bridge. Turn off

Symonds Street across the bridge, cross straight over Grafton Road at the traffic lights and walk past the hospital. The Domain gates are on the left. It is quite a long walk but most boaties are fit and it is a good chance to stretch your legs if you have been on your boat for some time. It is uphill going but at least it will be downhill for the return.

Buying books
There are several second-hand bookshops in the city, although some stock the more valuable rare books rather than cheap reading matter. Walk up High Street/Lorne Street, which runs parallel with Queen Street, to the east and you will find some. There is also one on the corner of Victoria and Albert Streets which specialises in science fiction. Opportunity shops usually have a few books too and there is one in Victoria Street West between Albert and Hobson Streets.

Auckland is also full of regular bookshops, many of which have specials and remainders, and on the first floor of the Downtown Shopping Centre there is a shop specialising in reduced price books.

Trans Pacific Marine, Quay Street, has a very wide selection of nautical books, guides and charts.

Swimming pools
There are outdoor pools at Point Erin, not far from the marina on the way to Ponsonby, and at Parnell, along the waterfront, and tepid pools on the way into Downtown from the marina.

Narrow Neck Beach, Devonport

Auckand City Art Gallery
The Auckland City Art Gallery is not far from the library and you could combine a visit to both. From the library, cross Wellesley Street towards the old building on the corner of Kitchener Street. The entrance is a little way down this road.

Entertainment
Auckland has many cinemas and theatres within walking distance of the marina. You could treat yourself to a taxi back to the boat. Concerts are held at the Town Hall. Local tourist papers such as the *Tourist Times* give full details. *Tourist Times* is available from the Aotea Square Information Centre, the Government Tourist Bureau at 99 Queen Street, and hotels and tourist shops.

Rangitoto Island

Facilities

Islands which are part of the Hauraki Gulf Maritime Park are mainly conservation sites and do not have services such as fuel, shops and repairs. However, they do provide a variety of other limited·resources.

 WATER   limited supply at Rangitoto wharf.

 RUBBISH DISPOSAL   bins at Yankee Wharf and Islington Bay.

 TOILETS   Islington Bay, Rangitoto Wharf, McKenzies Bay.

 RANGER   Islington Bay, Rangitoto Wharf (seasonal); telephone 727-674.

 BARBECUE SITES   Yankee Wharf (Islington Bay) and Rangitoto Wharf but check restrictions with ranger during closed fire season.

 TRANSPORT   there are regular ferry sailings to Rangitoto from Auckland.

 TELEPHONE   Islington Bay and Rangitoto Wharf.

 FIRST AID   Islington Bay Ranger Station, Rangitoto Wharf (seasonal).

The first island of the Hauraki Gulf Maritime Park reached from Auckland is Rangitoto, which is designated a scenic reserve. Its symmetrical cone is a familiar landmark to Aucklanders and can be seen from most parts of the city.

Rangitoto is an extinct volcano which last erupted around 200 years ago. The island is still volcanic rock with no soil in the usual sense and visitors should wear good protective shoes, particularly in summer when the ground becomes very hot.

There are several walks, the most popular being the summit walk with a magnificent view of the gulf from the top. Despite the lack of real soil there are many plants growing in fissures and the island is internationally known for the developing pohutukawa forest. There are large black-backed gull nesting colonies.

Before the Pakeha came Rangitoto was a parrot reserve for Chief Te Pereta. Maori have also used it as a burial ground and a wartime lookout.

The island has had several other uses. In 1892 a plant was set up to manufacture salt by evaporation

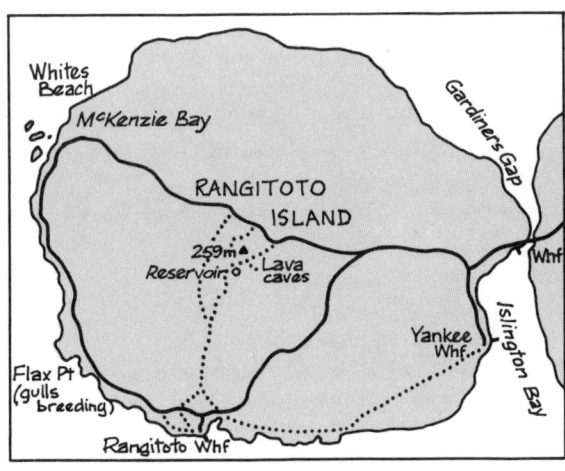

but the project failed. Then the volcanic lava was quarried from 1898 to 1930, the stone being used for Auckland's public works. Between 1925 and 1930 prison labour was used to build roads on the island. During the Second World War Rangitoto was declared a prohibited area and the summit was used as a base for harbour defence, fire control and radio station.

Once it was possible to have a holiday home on the island but this has now been stopped and as the owners of the few remaining baches die, the buildings are demolished.

Anchorage

Best known of the bays is Islington Bay/Izzie Bay/ Drunks Bay. It is so close to Auckland that it makes a good Friday night anchorage for a weekend cruise. The bay is between Rangitoto and Motutapu on the east side of the island. There are two wharves, Yankee Wharf and Islington Bay, and dinghies can land on the shore but beware the rocky nature of the coastline. Dogs are not allowed to land because it is a reserve.

Runabouts can land at Islington Bay, McKenzies Bay and Whites Beach.

Recreation

Beaches
Sand beaches at McKenzies and Whites Beach. All other beaches are basaltic rock. There are limited shellfish in Islington Bay and Gardiners Gap. There is not much shade from the sun ashore and because of the nature of the ground the heat of the sun reflects off the rock. If going ashore wear good

Islington Bay

footwear and a hat and take a drink if going for a walk.

Walks
There is a track around much of the island which passes old quarries, salt ponds and a breeding colony of black-backed gulls at Flax Point Bridge. This is where prisoners would bring a wire basket to catch their daily ration of fish.

The well-marked track to the summit starts at Rangitoto Wharf but there are also roads from Rangitoto Wharf and Islington Bay. Where the wharf track reaches some water tanks it branches to lava caves on the right. A loop track takes you around the summit, which is 259 m above sea-level. For the less energetic there are bush walks around Islington Bay and Rangitoto Wharf.

Motutapu Island

Facilities

 WATER limited supply at Home Bay.

 RUBBISH DISPOSAL bins provided at Islington Bay and Home Bay.

 TOILETS Islington Bay, Home Bay.

 RANGER Islington Bay (quarantine area) and Home Bay; telephone 727-674.

 TELEPHONE Islington Bay and Home Bay.

 FIRST AID all island safety services and first aid from Ranger Stations at Islington Bay and Home Bay.

 BARBECUE SITES Islington Bay and Home Bay but check restrictions during closed fire season.

 CAMPSITE Home Bay (see below).

 TRANSPORT ferry service from Auckland.

Alongside Rangitoto and joined to it by a causeway is Motutapu, meaning sacred island. The name is thought to have come from the first Polynesian explorers who named it after the last island they saw as they left Hawaiiki. It is the third largest reserve in the Hauraki Gulf Maritime Park and provides over 1500 hectares of recreation area, mainly grassland.

A wide range of evidence of Maori settlement has survived and more than 400 separate archaeological sites have been recorded, some dating back to the 12th century AD. The sites range from a sizeable fortified pa, as in Home Bay and Station Bay, to small camps where one or two families might have lived.

In 1842 Motutapu was purchased from the Maori and in 1869 it was bought by the Reid brothers who made it popular with ferries transporting picnickers from Auckland.

The island is now farmed by the Department of Conservation on behalf of the park and visitors have the chance to view the routine of farming life at close quarters. This could be of interest to overseas visitors who have heard all about our 70 million sheep and want to see some of them. There are also cattle.

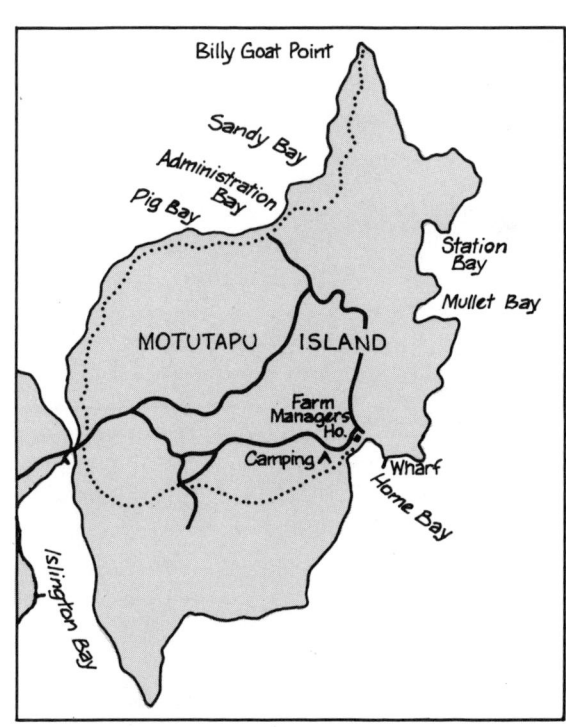

Islington Bay

Camping is allowed on the island and there are several anchorages with beaches. There are some good walks with magnificent views and much evidence of Second World War military activity, such as gun emplacements, which the public can visit. Look out for wallabies around the coastal cliffs.

Anchorage

Principal anchorages are Islington Bay, Home Bay, Station Bay, Mullet Bay, Waikalabubu Bay, Sandy Bay and Administration Bay. This range provides a bay for most conditions. Runabouts can land at all these bays.

Recreation

Beaches
Motutapu has sand/shingle beaches with safe swimming but take hats and sun-cream ashore as there are not many trees for shade.

Children will find plenty of space to run around and they will enjoy the farm animals. There are rock pools to explore in the bays at the northern end of the island.

Camping

The Park Board has developed a 50-site camping ground suitable for tents at Home Bay on the eastern side of the island. Campers are required to be fairly self-sufficient, but toilets, water, rubbish bins, barbecue sites and hangi sites are provided. No open fires or domestic pets are allowed. There is a limit of 14 days' stay. Bookings should be made by phoning the Senior Ranger, telephone 727-674.

Walks

The walk from Home Bay to Islington Bay is part of the New Zealand Walkway system. The round trip takes about three hours and crosses open farmland with spectacular views over the islands of the gulf and back to the mainland. It is easily graded and well marked with white-painted wooden posts.

Home Bay, Motutapu Island

An alternative return trip is via Administration Bay on the northern coast. This gives access to Billy Goat Point with its good fishing spots and Second World War fortifications. Large guns, magazines and radio huts can be seen at Administration Bay. The northern coast also has some good, sandy swimming beaches at Administration Bay, Pig Bay and Sandy Bay.

Motuihe Island

Facilities

 WATER   at Wharf Bay and Calypso Bay toilets.

 RUBBISH DISPOSAL   limited facilities, visitors are urged to take their own rubbish away with them.

 TOILETS/CHANGING SHED   at Wharf Bay next to canteen; toilet only at Calypso Bay.

 FARM PARK MANAGER   first house up the hill from the canteen; telephone 534-8095.

 TELEPHONE   no public telephone.

 FIRST AID   Farm Park Manager is trained in first aid.

 BARBECUE SITES   six barbecue sites.

 PICNIC AREAS   the picnic grounds may be booked by organised groups; telephone 727-671.

 CANTEEN   hot and cold food and drinks and boating provisions. Catering service; telephone 534-8095 for enquiries.

 TRANSPORT   regular ferry service from Auckland.

Motuihe is one of the most popular islands because of its proximity to Auckland and accessibility by regular ferry service. Up to 4000 people a day visit the island in summer so if you want to get away from it all this is not the place.

However, if you want good walks, sandy beaches with shelter in most winds and the added bonus of a canteen serving hot and cold foods then Motuihe *is* the place to go.

Like Motutapu, Motuihe is farmed on behalf of the Park Board and carries an average of 1000 breeding ewes and 300 dry stock. The public are able to see a working farm at first hand.

The island was originally called Te-Motu-O-Ihenga after the nephew of the navigator of the Arawa canoe, one of the first canoes to arrive in New Zealand. The island remained in Maori hands until 1839 and there are about 30 archaeological sites showing the location of storage pits, whares and defensive ditches. Metal signs mark the location of these sites with the best example at Pah Point near Guys Cliff. See map.

Today Motuihe is a happy place where people go to enjoy themselves. However, it has not always been that way. Previous users of the island longed to leave it. In 1872 the Crown bought the island to use as a quarantine station. Its heaviest period of use was in the 1918 flu epidemic and the graves on the island belong to those who died from the disease.

During the First World War Motuihe was used as a prisoner-of-war camp, the most famous of the prisoners being the German Count Felix von Luckner who made a daring escape. He was recaptured and returned to the island, but his exploits during his escape made him famous.

Motuihe served as a children's health camp and a naval training establishment before becoming part of the Hauraki Gulf Maritime Park in 1967.

Anchorage

Motuihe is a triangular shape with sheltered anchorages on each side of the triangle at Wharf Bay, Ocean Beach, Snapper Bay and Calypso Bay.

Ferries use the wharf on the north-western end of the island. Landing for dinghies is no problem on the sandy beach although the tide goes out for some distance on the west side. No domestic animals allowed.

Runabouts can land on all beaches but remember the state of the tide on the west side as you may have a long haul to get back into the water when the tide goes out.

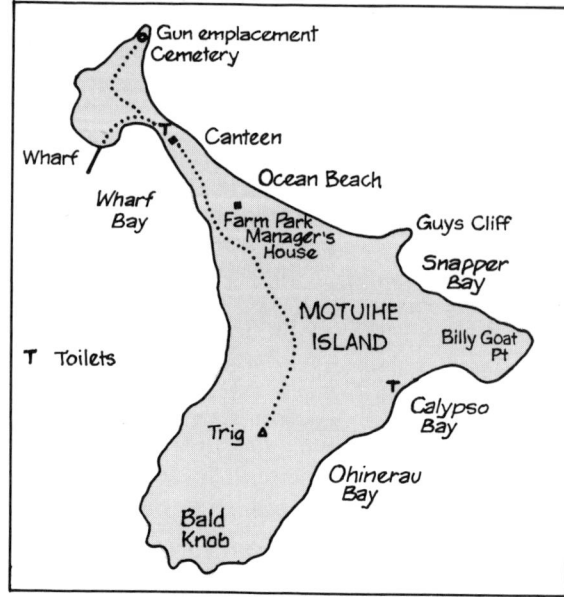

Recreation

Beaches

The beaches are sandy and shallow, ideal for swimming, skiing, snorkelling and for young children to splash around in. Pohutukawa and pine trees provide shade from the sun. The two beaches at the northern point of the island are separated by 50 m of sand dunes so one or other is always protected from the wind.

There are rock pools for the children to explore on the north-eastern side of the island at low tide. Mussels, tuatua, cockles and kina will also be found at low tide.

Walks

The contour of the island is easy with excellent walks for all ages. There are trees along the coast but the walks are across more open land so take some sun protection.

From the wharf to Calypso Bay and back is approximately two hours and round the island three hours, but allow extra time and stop for a picnic at whichever beach is most sheltered.

Vantage points at Bald Knob, Billy Goat Point, Guys Cliff and Cemetery Point give wonderful views over the Gulf.

The cemetery containing the graves of the flu victims is on the northernmost tip of the island. Head in a northerly direction from the canteen. It is also the site of a wartime gun emplacement.

Look out for the rare New Zealand dotterel which nests along the coast.

Waiheke Island

Facilities

 FUEL at garage in Belgium Street, Ostend, Oneroa Service Station, Onetangi Service Station.

 GAS BOTTLES refilled at the hardware shop, Belgium Street, Ostend.

 WATER at Matiatia.

 STORES supermarket in Ostend Road and dairy and vegetable shop in Belgium Street. Seven-day grocery store, butcher, dairy and book swap in Miami Road, Surfdale. There is also a big range of shops across the island at Oneroa. It is within walking distance but there are buses too.

 TELEPHONE at post offices in Surfdale and Ostend.

 POLICE Waikare Road, Oneroa. Telephone Waiheke 8777.

 REPAIRS flat-bottomed boats can dry out in the inlet where the boat club is located. There is a grid on the starboard inlet for keel boats to 1.8 m draught. The hardware shop in Ostend has a limited selection of marine fittings.

 POSTAL Belgium Street, Ostend. Miami Road, Surfdale.

 EATING OUT nearest to Putiki Bay is the take-away shop and ice-cream parlour in Ostend and the take-away shop in Surfdale. There is also a selection of coffee shops, restaurants and take-aways in Oneroa.

 TRANSPORT regular ferries run from Matiatia to Auckland. The vehicular ferry runs from Kennedys Point to Panmure up the Tamaki River. Local bus service around the eastern end of the island which meets the ferries at Matiatia. Amphibian service between Surfdale and Auckland.

 ACCOMMODATION selection of motels and cabins.

Waiheke is the largest and most populated island in the Hauraki Gulf. It covers an area of 9324 hectares with 96 km of coastline. Many residents commute by ferry to Auckland each day. It is not part of the Maritime Park so landing is unrestricted.

The narrower western end of the island is the most populated and served by ferries to Matiatia and Kennedys Point. The eastern end is not so developed and there are several quiet bays on the coast.

As the islands of the Hauraki Gulf Maritime Park do not have any services such as fuel, shops and repairs, Waiheke is the place to go if you are on a cruise and need such facilities. The stores and supplies are in the residential settlements on the western end of the island. There are no facilities on the eastern end.

Putiki Bay on the south coast is a good bay for a provisioning and recreation stop as it is close to the settlements of Ostend and Surfdale. The bay is sheltered from all but south-west winds. However, there is no wharf so everything has to be transported by dinghy. The vehicular ferry berths at Kennedy Point in the outer part of Putiki Bay.

Matiatia Bay on the western end has water and road access to the rest of the island, but it is not a good place to stay for long as the ferries serving the island, including a 33 m catamaran which creates a very big wash, call into the bay regularly.

While Putiki Bay is good for provisioning there are many more anchorages on Waiheke depending on the wind direction. However, there are no facilities at most of the bays. *The Royal Akarana Yacht Club Coastal Cruising Handbook* has full details.

Anchorage

Putiki Bay has three parts divided by two headlands. There is a beacon off the end of the left-hand headland – Putiki Point – and the anchorage for keel boats is to port of the beacon. Enter the bay between Kennedys Point and the island, not between the two islands, and keep clear of an

Oneroa, Waiheke Island

unmarked rock just beyond the ferry wharf, especially if anchoring off the first beach in the bay.

Landing for dinghies is either on the main beach

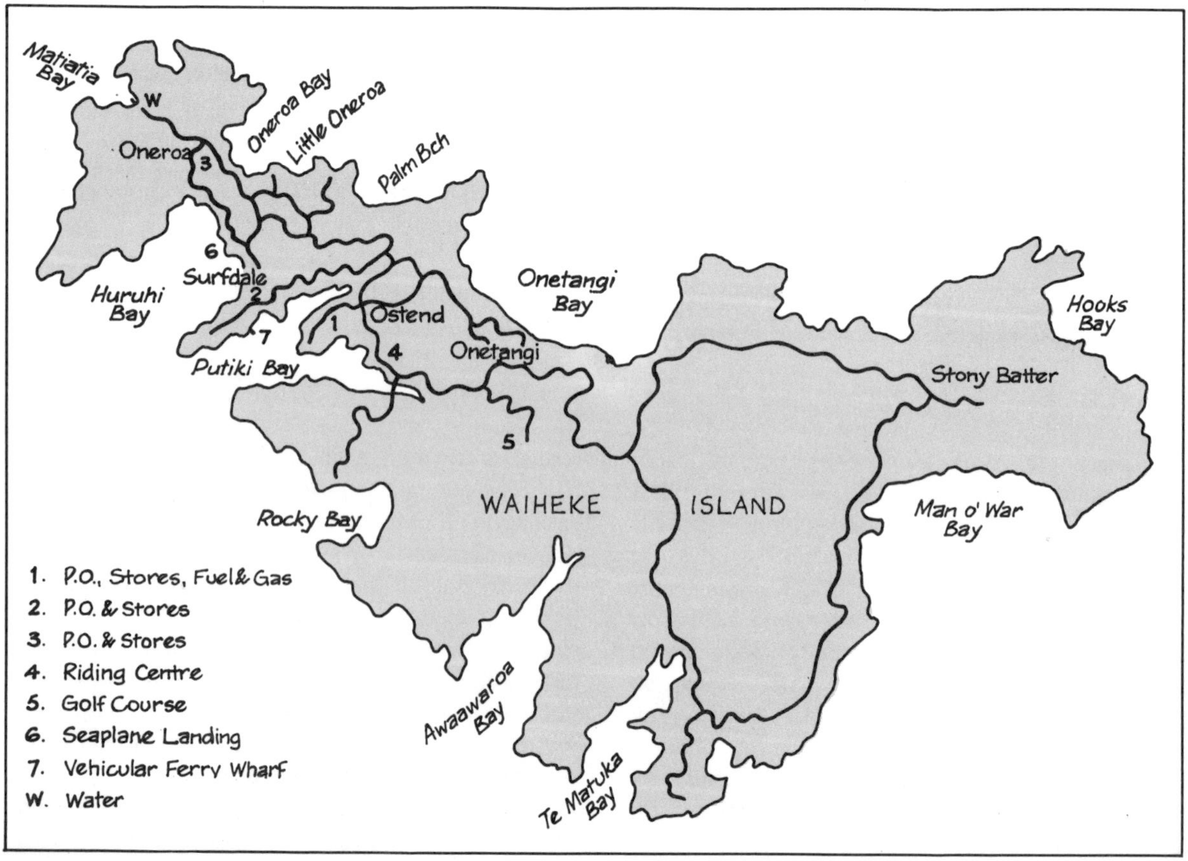

1. P.O., Stores, Fuel & Gas
2. P.O. & Stores
3. P.O. & Stores
4. Riding Centre
5. Golf Course
6. Seaplane Landing
7. Vehicular Ferry Wharf
W. Water

Oneroa Bay, Waiheke

or on the two headlands which stick out into the bay. The beach dries extensively at low tide so it is a long haul with the dinghy, but it is the closest landing place to Surfdale. The farthest headland to the right is the most convenient landing place for the Ostend shops. There is room for several dinghies on the small landing area, but watch for old wharf piles under the water.

The middle inlet dries extensively at its head and is very popular with multi-hulls, which can take the ground without any problem. Runabouts can also go in there.

Recreation

Beaches

Putiki Bay itself does not have a very good beach as it dries extensively and becomes muddy. Surfdale next door is better, but the best beaches are on the northern coast. Oneroa, Little Oneroa, Palm Beach and Onetangi are magnificent sandy beaches and worth the effort of getting there while anchored in Putiki.

Little Oneroa, as the name suggests, is a small version of the big beach. It is a little cove with plenty of trees for shade. Oneroa also has trees but Onetangi is more open and has houses along the beach front. All are good for swimming, snorkelling and playing on the beach.

Walks

The whole island is open to walkers and you can choose whether you walk through the residential area, along country roads or along the beaches. The residential areas are interesting for the variety of houses.

Waiheke is partly a dormitory suburb of Auckland and there are some palatial permanent homes. Beside them are little baches which have been providing holiday accommodation for years. In between these two extremes are many interesting houses. These residential roads have views of the sea and large areas of bush and gardens between the houses.

Animals graze in the open country towards the east. There is one official walk, Stony Batter, which is part of the New Zealand Walkways system. It covers former defence land where the remains of three Second World War gun sites still exist. The gun emplacements are connected by underground passages which also provide access between underground offices, machine rooms and magazines. Take a torch. For boaties without road transport the nearest anchorages to Stony Batter are Man O' War Bay and Hooks Bay on the eastern end of the island.

Museum

The island history is preserved in documents, photographs and artefacts housed in the Waiheke Historical Society's museum at Ostend near the shops.

Sports

Horse-riding – there is a horse-riding centre just along the road from Oneroa towards Rocky Bay at Shepherds Point.

Golf – the nine-hole golf course is on the road between Putiki Bay and Onetangi.

Tennis – visitors are welcome on the courts at Ostend Reserve and Rocky Bay.

Roller-skating – there is a roller-skating rink at Surfdale with day and evening sessions.

Ruthe Passage

Ruthe Passage runs between the eastern end of Waiheke and the islands of Pakatoa, Rotoroa and Ponui. The sea can develop quite a nasty roll through the passage and an additional problem is the wash created by the regular catamaran ferry service to the holiday resort of Pakatoa. The wash does not actually reach the shore until some time after the ferry has passed so be aware of this problem, particularly if launching a dinghy.

Ponui Island

Ponui is privately owned and farmed and has a few farm houses. It has some good anchorages. Most popular is North Harbour which has shelter from all but northerlies. There is a sandy beach for landing and for children to play and there is also a walk up the headland on the western side of the bay which gives views over Ruthe Passage to Waiheke.

Just around the headland to the east of North Harbour is a long beach, a good picnic spot. If you have a keel boat it is probably easier to leave the boat safety anchored in North Harbour and take the dinghy as there is not much water in the bay. Runabouts and shallow-draught boats will find enough water. There are a few trees to provide shade. We have been on this beach when there has been no other boat in sight – like being on a desert island!

If a northerly comes up while you are anchored in North Harbour, Rotoroa directly opposite provides shelter. Take a bearing during daylight in case you need to move after dark because there are some rocks off the island.

Rotoroa is used by the Salvation Army as a rehabilitation centre for alcoholics and can cater for up to 70 people with a staff of about 20. The public are not allowed to land on the island.

Pakatoa Island

Pakatoa is a holiday resort. It was bought by Sir Robert Kerridge in 1964 and is now part of the Pacer/Kerridge group which owns entertainment facilities such as cinemas and bowling centres. It has chalet-style accommodation with recreational facilities such as swimming-pool, tennis courts, nine-hole golf course and bowling green. There is a fully licensed restaurant, lounge bar and snack bar and some nights there is a disco.

Pakatoa has its own yacht club which provides moorings, fuel and water for members and use of the facilities on the island, including showers and laundry.

Tiritiri Matangi Island

Facilities

 WATER for hand washing only at toilets.

 RUBBISH DISPOSAL take all rubbish away.

 TOILETS at wharf landing.

 TELEPHONE emergency telephone only.

 FIRST AID Conservation Officer.

 BARBECUE *no* fires allowed.

Heading north, the next island belonging to the Park is Tiritiri Matangi. It is situated off the end of the Whangaparaoa Peninsula and boats heading for Kawau Island will pass between the peninsula and Tiritiri Matangi.

Tiritiri Matangi is a particularly interesting island as it is an 'open sanctuary', where anyone willing to treat the island with respect has free access to see endangered plant and animal life in its naural environment.

Because of the fragile nature of the island no fires are allowed. On such a small island, one fire out of control would be devastating and undo all the hard work of hundreds of volunteers who have planted trees.

The World Wildlife Fund New Zealand made Tiritiri Matangi one of its primary projects and initiated a fund-raising drive which made a re-vegetation programme possible. Thousands of native trees have been planted to support a growing number of reintroduced bird species.

A nursery was established in 1983 to produce 30 000 trees and shrubs a year from seed gathered on the island. Visitors are welcome to have a look round the nursery and anyone interested in helping with the planting programme should contact the Park Board Information Officer, telephone (09) 799-972. Transport can be arranged.

Lighthouse

Tiritiri Matangi is perhaps best known for its lighthouse which stands as a sentinel at the entrance to Auckland and may be visited. Today the 20.5 m-high lighthouse is painted .white and automatic. However, it has an interesting history.

In the early days of New Zealand's settlement the number of ships calling at Auckland increased and there was a need for some warning of the dangers such as Flat Rock and Shearer Rock. It was decided to build a lighthouse on the island and materials were ordered from England in 1863. The whale-oil lamp was lit for the first time on 21 December 1864 and the grand unveiling was held on New Year's Day 1865. In those days the lighthouse was painted bright red and there were two keepers who grazed sheep and cattle in the surrounding reserve. The original houses are now gone, replaced in the 1920s with the present houses.

The light became automatic for the first time in 1935 when an acetylene-burning automatic fixed light was installed. The keepers were no longer required and the light operated as a signal station only until 1947 when the keepers were reinstated and the tower painted white.

The light was electrified in 1955, powered by a diesel generator, but an underwater main power cable was laid in 1967 when the light was linked to the national power grid. In April 1984 it was automated for the second time in its history.

Anchorage

Tiritiri is more suitable for day trips than as an overnight anchorage. It could be a stop off on the way to or from Kawau Island. No domestic animals are allowed ashore.

The wharf on the south-west point of the island may be used for loading and unloading passengers and there are anchorages at Hobbs Bay and Fishermans Bay. There is also a mooring buoy for visitors' use. Beware of the power cable at Hobbs Bay.

Landing for runabouts at Hobbs Bay.

Recreation

Beaches

Sandy shallow beaches suitable for swimming and snorkelling, and trees for shade. Rock pools to explore.

Walks

There are several walking tracks giving visitors the opportunity to explore areas of the island that provide both scenic and wildlife interest. Some tracks are steep, rising to 70 m above sea-level, so a reasonable standard of fitness is required.

Please keep to the tracks as much as possible as scientific studies are being carried out on the island. Among the birds likely to be found are saddlebacks, tuis, bellbirds and red-crowned parakeets.

Saddle Island

Saddle Island

This is a small islet off the end of the Mahurangi Peninsula north of Tiritiri Matangi Island. It is a popular day anchorage and landing for runabouts and there is a large sandy beach on the western side with pohutukawa trees for shade. Visitors are asked to take care, if walking inland, not to disturb the burrows of fluttering shearwaters. No domestic pets allowed. Beware of the extensive reef at the northern tip of the island, particularly if making for Kawau.

Mahurangi Harbour

Diagram of Mahurangi River available from Rodney Country Council, Centreway Road, Orewa.

The Mahurangi Harbour is about 60 km north of Auckland by road on the east coast and not far from several islands of the Hauraki Gulf including Kawau. It has several inlets which provide shelter and the Mahurangi River runs up to the small township of Warkworth where supplies can be obtained.

The harbour is formed by the mainland (Mahurangi West, reached by road off State Highway 1 just north of Orewa) and a peninsula (Mahurangi East) which begins at Warkworth and includes Snells Beach, Algies Bay and Martins Bay on the eastern seaward coast.

There are some interesting places to visit and children can sail their dinghies or practise rowing in the inlets. Apart from Casnell Island and the Auckland Regional Authority reserves at Big Bay, Te Muri, Sullivans Bay and Meter Bay there is no restriction on landing with domestic pets.

Facilities

Sullivans Bay has toilets, camping facilities, a ranger, and a telephone. Scotts Landing has toilets, a rubbish bin, and a grid for hull cleaning. All other facilities are at Warkworth, for boats which can get up the river (see page 69).

Anchorage

At the entrance to the harbour on the west side are several beaches suitable for day anchorages, including the Auckland Regional Authority reserve at Sullivans Bay. There is road access to the reserve and Opahi Bay if you want to meet friends and take them out to the boat.

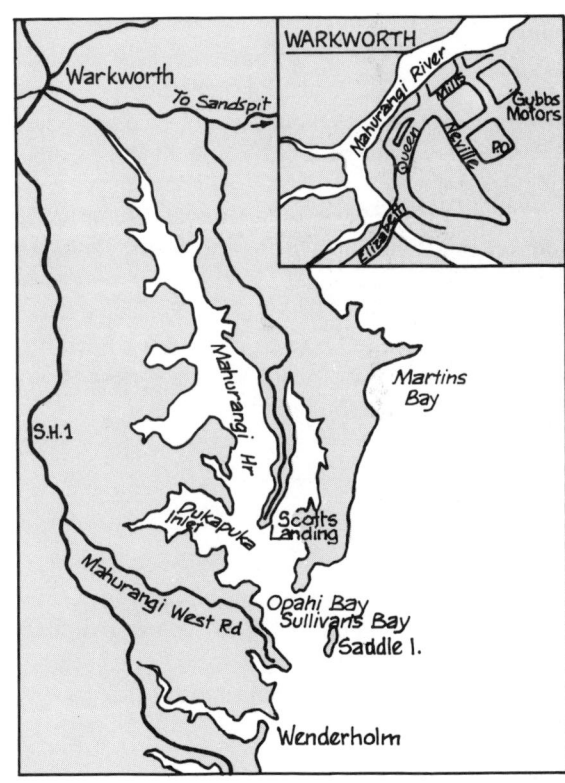

For overnight anchorage move further into the harbour past the large area of permanent moorings. The inlet on the port side is Pukapuka. It shallows out considerably at its head and there are oyster racks to watch out for, but there is a good clear anchorage in the lee of the headland to starboard.

Do not go in too close to the shore as it is rocky

in parts and there is also a sandbank about half-way along which dries leaving a small lagoon at low tide – a good spot for pipis. Keep an eye on your depth sounder or leadline and be guided by the few permanent moorings.

There is room for anchoring behind the permanent moorings in the main river off Scotts Landing, but the tidal flow is strong and when wind and tide are against each other it makes this position very rocky.

An unsealed road ends at Scotts Landing. There is no longer a wharf but fishing boats tie up alongside the wall. A street light on the shore offers some guidance at night.

Another anchorage is in the inlet to starboard of Casnell Island, but again be guided by your depth sounder as it shallows out considerably at its head. The best shelter is in the lee of the Cantyre Peninsula.

Shallow-draught boats can make the trip up the Mahurangi River at high tide to Warkworth. The channel is marked but the river is very muddy and silted up on bends so take it carefully. There is room for several boats at Warkworth and the anchorage is beside the shopping centre which makes it very convenient for provisioning.

Launching ramps

Warkworth
Dawsons Point
Scotts Landing – at the end of the Cantyre Peninsula (Mahurangi East) along a metalled road. Small parking area.
Opahi Bay – small parking area.

Recreation

Beaches

The sandy beaches are at the entrance to the harbour and quite exposed so it is best to make a day trip to the beach and then return to a more sheltered anchorage at night. The beaches at Sullivans Bay, the Auckland Regional Authority

Mahurangi Harbour

reserve, have facilities for picnickers including toilets and drinking water. It is only a short distance to some of the islands for a bit of variety.

In Pukapuka inlet water covers most of the shore at high tide so if you are planning a picnic or barbecue, time it between the tides. Further up the river the shore is mangrove and is not good for landing.

Between Scotts Landing and Casnell Island there is a sandy beach which is part of the causeway to the island.

Walks

Casnell Island, part of the Hauraki Gulf Maritime Park, is worth a visit. In pre-European times it was an island pa. It is now joined to the mainland by a causeway accessible only at low tide. Around the island is a sedimentary rock shelf which has many rock pools suitable for exploring at low tide. No domestic animals allowed.

If you have a dog with you then you can walk in the opposite direction away from Casnell Island along the Mahurangi East road. The road follows the narrow peninsula and there are views both sides, to the harbour and the open sea. Along this road is the Burton Wells reserve which stretches from the roadway to the river. If you have young children who are restricted by road walking then take them into the reserve where they can have a good run around and climb a few trees. There are no facilities.

Warkworth

Facilities

 FUEL garages.

 GAS BOTTLES Europa garage in main street.

 WATER on river bank.

 STORES wide selection of shops including two supermarkets, butcher, bread and cake shop, vegetable shop, clothing stores, and suppliers of sports goods, second-hand boating gear, fishing equipment, hardware and books. The second-hand shop above the pottery shop has used paperbacks if you want to stock up the ship's library.
Banks – several major banks represented.

 RUBBISH DISPOSAL bins on river bank.

 TOILETS next to council building on riverside.

 TELEPHONE at post office.

 POLICE Elizabeth Street, telephone Warkworth 8109.

 FIRST AID telephone numbers of doctors and vet in the telephone directory.

 REPAIRS boat builder with all facilities   ɔre along the river before the town is reached.

 POST OFFICE is in Neville Street.

 EATING OUT there are several restaurants, take-away bars, coffee shops and ice-cream parlours to choose from.

 CINEMA see local paper for details.

 TRANSPORT Gubbs Motors is the depot for bus services to Auckland and Northland; telephone Warkworth 8348.

Warkworth is accessible at high tide by boats up to 1.5 m draught. The grassy river bank is a good place for a picnic – if the ducks will let you eat. There are plenty of tables provided. If you want shade, walk across the bridge and there is a picnic area underneath trees, conveniently near an ice-cream parlour! There is also a children's playground by the river. As you go up the river you will pass the old cement works ruins. These are open to the public.

Motuora Island

Motuora Island, four miles east of Mahurangi Harbour, is an attractive farm which, like Motuihe and Motutapu, is run on behalf of the Maritime Park. Besides enjoying the usual island attractions such as walks and beaches the public may camp there. The camping ground is on the west coast near the resident caretaker's house and permits are available from the Kawau Island Senior Conservation Officer, telephone Kawau 882.

Fresh water and toilets are provided and possible activities include water-skiing, walking, swimming, fishing and skin-diving. There is no ferry service to the island so campers have to get there by private boat.

Kawau Island

Chart No: 5227 Cape Rodney to Motuora Island
Chart No: 5321 Kawau Island to Rangitoto Island
Map No: Infomap 260 No R09

Facilities

Most facilities are at the Kawau Island Yacht Club in Bon Accord Harbour, the white building to port half-way down the harbour. It has a long jetty with fuel pumps and water. It costs only a few dollars to join the club and one subscription covers the whole crew. This gives access to the following services:

 FUEL   on wharf.

 WATER   on wharf.

 STORES   including bread, meat, frozen goods, dog food, baby food, ice-creams, souvenirs and film, books and magazines.

 TOILETS/SHOWERS   separate facilities for men and women. Coin operated meters.

 LAUNDRY   two agitator-type machines with wringer, two tubs with hot and cold water and a drier. Pay at the shop.

 TELEPHONE   public phone box open at all times. No charge for calls on the Warkworth exchange; all other calls have to be transfer charge or collect.

 POSTAL   members can send and receive mail in the yacht club's mail bag which is collected and delivered by the ferry. Check the collection days at the club.

Other facilities on the island are:

 WATER   on the main wharf at Mansion House Bay. Access to the wharf is only for taking on water as it is busy with ferries bringing visitors to Kawau.

 RUBBISH DISPOSAL   Mansion House Bay. There is a rubbish trailer provided by the Hauraki Gulf Maritime Park.

 TOILETS   Mansion House Bay.

 HARBOUR-MASTER   Gordon Johnston, Camp Bentzon, North Cove, telephone 807.

 REPAIRS   Ian McIntyre, Smelting House Bay, is able to help with small repairs. Ian operates from the boat shed in the bay but if he is not there his house is on the right at the very end of the beach. The boat-yard has a trolley for hauling out and a grid for cleaning down. Parts can be sent over by ferry if necessary.

 DIVE AIR   Ian McIntyre, Smelting House Bay.

 TEA-ROOMS AND SOUVENIRS   Mansion House Bay.

 ICE   Ian McIntyre, Smelting House Bay.

 FRESH VEGETABLES   sometimes available from Ian McIntyre, Smelting House Bay.

PUMP   available for fire fighting or pumping out holed boats. Contact the harbour-master.

 CONSERVATION OFFICERS   Hauraki Gulf Maritime Park Senior Conservation Officer: telephone 882 or 867.

 TRANSPORT   *Ferry* – there is a regular service between Kawau Island and Sandspit just out of Warkworth on the mainland. To check on times and arrange pick up from one of the jetties, telephone Warkworth 8006

(Fullers) or Warkworth 7307 (Mansion House Ferries).

Taxis – the ferry driver can arrange for the taxi to meet you at Sandspit for the short trip to Warkworth and there will probably be others making the journey who can share the cost. Taxi telephone is Warkworth 8748.

Bus services – buses leave Warkworth for Auckland and Northland. For timetable telephone Gubbs Motors Warkworth 8348. They are also the agents for Newmans and New Zealand Road Services.

Kawau Island is a bush-covered island just off the coast and very popular with Aucklanders for weekend trips.

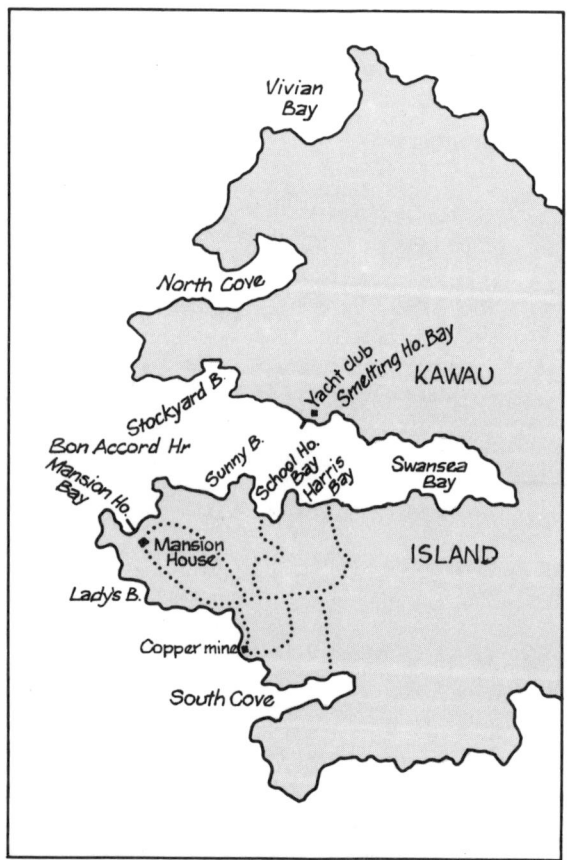

Kawau's two main harbours are on the west side. Bon Accord Harbour is the larger of the two with many separate bays giving shelter in all conditions. North Cove, at the north end of the island, is almost land-locked, but dries out in its upper reaches.

Other anchorages are Vivian Bay in the north, which has the only good beach on the island, and South Cove with the copper mine ruins. There is no anchorage on the east coast, which is very exposed.

Kawau has a small permanent population, mainly retired or self-employed people who enjoy the solitude to pursue their crafts. Most of the residents have no road access to their properties; they come and go by ferry or private boat. There is a good ferry service to Kawau and the same boat takes the mail and supplies.

If you want to make the trip to Sandspit to shop in your own boat rather than by ferry it is possible to hire a mooring at Sandspit while you are shopping. Contact Tim Lees, telephone Warkworth 8811 or Fullers, telephone 8006. There is a strong current in the river and a bar at the entrance so work the tides and check your chart. Tim Lees is also able to fill gas bottles.

Anchorages

North Cove

This harbour is very tidal and deep-draught boats should not anchor beyond the line of permanent moorings. The western side has the most shelter but the wind can funnel into the bay over the hills. However, because it is almost land-locked, North Cove does offer shelter from any rough seas.

All the property around North Cove is private which makes landing a problem. What looks like a reserve area to starboard as you enter is Camp Bentzon, a camp used mainly by school parties but available also to other groups. However, it is not for the general public to use for landing. Beware of a reef, not marked on the chart, which extends from Camp Bentzon and when turning into North Cove from the south give the headland a good offing. Don't follow the ferry, which takes a short cut through a gap in the rocks!

Kawau Island ferry

Bon Accord

There are several anchorages in Bon Accord Harbour. The first on the south side is Mansion House Bay and easily recognisable by the grand mansion house, once the home of Sir George Grey. This bay is part of the Hauraki Gulf Maritime Park so pets are not permitted on shore.

Schoolhouse Bay, further along the harbour, is a good anchorage, although a roll develops in a strong westerly, despite the apparent shelter from that direction. Landing is at the main wharf and there is a track to Mansion House Bay and the copper mine ruins.

Around the corner from Schoolhouse Bay is Harris Bay which has a good beach for landing. However, there are a few old unmarked moorings which could snag anchors. If you do have this trouble, Gordon Johnston, the harbour-master, can arrange recovery of your anchor.

Opposite Schoolhouse Bay on the northern side of the harbour is Smelting House Bay beside the Kawau Island Yacht Club. The club has three mooring buoys in the bay for members, but if these are in use there is no problem with anchoring. Landing within the bay is easy or you can go direct to the yacht club wharf or ramp.

Stockyard Bay on the north side near the entrance slopes away quite sharply and an anchor can drag free down this slope. There are also some unmarked sunken moorings east of the wharf.

Vivian Bay

This bay has the best beach on Kawau Island so is good for children. There is good shelter from south-west through south to north-east and the mooring line is well defined. There are no public facilities and all the property in the bay is privately owned.

South Cove

Beware of the ground in this anchorage. It is fouled by weed and the old spoil from the copper mine.

Launching ramps

There are no launching ramps on Kawau Island, but runabouts and trailer sailers can be launched on the mainland opposite Kawau.

Recreation

Kawau Island is about the same size as Norfolk Island. Ten per cent of the land belongs to the Hauraki Gulf Maritime Park; Mansion House Bay and facilities are the main attraction. The rest of the land is privately owned.

The first documented visit by a European to Kawau was that of the Reverend Samuel Marsden in 1820. The island was sold in 1830 to a land company who transported kauri back to England and Australia for ships' spars. The sailors on the boats took back tales of green-blue stains on the rock indicating copper deposits and in the 1840s copper mining began.

Mining was soon a thriving industry and the population increased to between 400 and 500 people including wives and children. Reminders of these days remain in the ruins of the smelting house around the corner from the yacht club and the copper mine chimney at Dispute Cove.

Mansion House

In 1862 the Governor of New Zealand, Sir George Grey, bought the island and transformed the mine manager's cottage into the Mansion House almost as you see it today. The verandahs were added by a later owner. Grey introduced many species of exotic plants and animals including the wallabies which still run all over the island.

Mansion House, Kawau Island

Mansion House is open to visitors from 9.30 a.m. to 3.30 p.m. daily, admission adults $3, children $1. It has been furnished as it was in Grey's time and contains many of his own books and artefacts. One chair has carved animal heads which when twisted make the chair recline – the original lazyboy! One of the bedrooms houses a pictorial record of Kawau Island.

The grounds of the Mansion House form the recreation area for the bay. There is a kiosk serving light meals from 10 a.m. to 3 p.m. in summer (reduced hours in winter), picnic tables, barbecues and toilets.

Tracks

From Mansion House Bay there is a walk – one and a half hour round trip – via the copper mine look-out (20 minutes from Mansion House), copper mine ruins (15 minutes from look-out with a choice of Miners Track, Dispute Cove Track or Copper Mine Track) and the Redwood Track back to Mansion House.

Ladies Bay, just along the track from Mansion House, is a sheltered cove with a gently shelving beach, ideal for swimming. At high tide the water comes right up to the cliff.

An alternative walk from Mansion House is the track to Schoolhouse Bay. It is well defined and suitable for all ages, the only steep part being the last drop down into Schoolhouse Bay. A side-track leads to a graveyard which contains the graves of early settlers. Schoolhouse Bay is so named because it was the site of the schoolhouse for the children of Governor Grey's staff.

Schoolhouse Bay is the most populated bay on the island. On mail days there is quite a crowd on the wharf to collect mail and supplies delivered by the ferry.

There are tracks on other parts of the island but they are through private property so please respect this. The vegetation is mostly manuka and is home to the wallabies so look out for them, particularly at dusk when they are waking up.

Great Barrier Island

Chart No: 522 Bream Tail to Kawau Island including Great Barrier Island
Chart No: 5225 Great Barrier Island Ports and Anchorages, Tryphena Harbour
Map No: Infomap Holidaymaker No: 259

Facilities

 FUEL   Mulberry Grove store, Tryphena, Claris garage, Whangaparapara wharf, Port Fitzroy wharf.

 GAS BOTTLES   Port Fitzroy store, Mulberry Grove store, Tryphena, and Claris garage.

 WATER   Port Fitzroy wharf, Whangaparapara wharf.

 STORES   general stores at Port Fitzroy, Whangaparapara and Tryphena but supplies limited and may be short during busy holiday periods. Well-stocked store at Orama religious community, Karaka Bay, Port Abercrombie.

 RUBBISH DISPOSAL   main wharf, Port Fitzroy, Whangaparapara wharf, Department of Conservation pontoon and camping ground.

 TOILETS   above wharf, Port Fitzroy; Department of Conservation camping ground, Port Fitzroy; above wharf, Whangaparapara; Shoal Bay wharf.

 CONSERVATION OFFICER   Department of Conservation headquarters, Port Fitzroy; telephone PTF 4K.

 TELEPHONE   at shop above main wharf.

 POLICE AND COAST GUARD   telephone Claris 11.

 FIRST AID   public health nurse above wharf in Port Fitzroy; telephone PTF 6.

 REPAIRS   grid at Smokehouse Bay, Port Fitzroy. Department of Conservation slipway at headquarters is available for boats up to about 9 m. Fee charged.

 POSTAL   post offices at Port Fitzroy, Claris.

 LOCAL RADIO   Great Barrier radio listening on VHF 16 0700 to 2200hrs daily, SSB 2045kh 0900-0930, 1230-1245, 1700-1730 and 2030-2100 and CB Ch 12 0700-2200 hrs daily.

 INFORMATION   for further information contact the Information Centres at Port Fitzroy, Tryphena Travel Centre, or Department of Conservation, on arrival at Great Barrier.

 DIVE AIR   Great Barrier Charters, Port Fitzroy wharf, R. Kelsey, Whangaparapara wharf, Tryphena store.

 TRANSPORT   **by air:** Sea Bee Air (amphibian), telephone Auckland (09) 774-406; Great Barrier Airlines, telephone Auckland (09) 275-9120; 275-6612; and local aero clubs.
by sea: Sea Flight Cruises Ltd, telephone Auckland 366-1421; Trans Gulf (passenger

vehicle barge), telephone Auckland (09) 734-036 (after hours Auckland (09) 456-691).

 ACCOMMODATION there are several guest houses and lodges on the island.

Great Barrier Island is the North Island's largest offshore island, covering an area of 28 000 hectares, and was so named by Captain Cook because of the protection it gives to the Hauraki Gulf. It lies to the north-east of the Coromandel Peninsula, separated from the mainland by Colville Channel.

There is a permanent population of between 900 and 1000 and increasing mainly around the settlements of Port Fitzroy, Whangaparapara, Claris and Tryphena. Many Ngatiwai are returning to their ancestral lands around Katherine Bay. The residents make a living from farming, fishing, forestry or horticulture and such things as crafts and tourism.

Today there is no large-scale industry but in the past there has been mining and logging. The mining was short-lived, most of the Cornish miners moving on to Great Barrier after the mines on Kawau Island failed.

In 1910 the Kauri Timber Company built what was at the time the largest sawmill in the Southern Hemisphere at Whangaparapara. Gum-digging was also a big industry in earlier times. Reminders of this past activity can be found on the island. The concrete foundations of a stamping battery established during the mining era are beside the road to Whangaparapara. Trams brought the gold- and silver-bearing quartz to the battery where it was crushed. The crushings were then washed down terraces and the valuable metals precipitated out by amalgamation with mercury.

Evidence of the timber industry are the piles from the sawmill wharf at Whangaparapara and three kauri dams across the Kaiarara Stream. The lowest dam is the largest and was built with the aid of machinery carried up in pieces and reassembled on site. Water was allowed to build up behind the dams, and then released suddenly to flood kauri logs downstream to the river mouth. There is a walk to the dams. See 'Walks' on pp. 78–81.

Great Barrier Island is very popular with Auckland boaties in the holiday season. It is about 60 miles from Auckland and many people head for Kawau

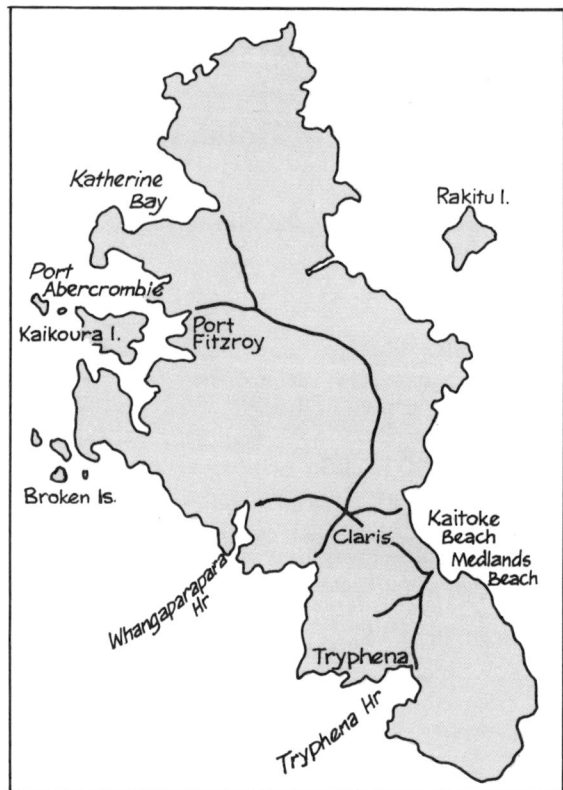

Island first then sail across to Great Barrier. Activities for boaties include diving, snorkelling, surfing, fishing, walking and camping.

There are several sheltered deep-water anchorages on the west coast, the main ones at Port Fitzroy and Whangaparapara. The east coast is more open – there is no more land before Chile – but there are some lovely sandy beaches. The interior of the island is mostly forest and bush with many walks.

Anchorage

The most popular anchorages are found at Port Fitzroy, which is almost land-locked by Kaikoura

Port Fitzroy, Great Barrier Island

Island. The shop and Department of Conservation headquarters are in Rarohara Bay. Much of the land around Port Fitzroy is part of the Great Barrier Forest administered by the Department of Conservation.

Some of the inlets dry at their heads including Kaiarara Bay, Kiwiriki Bay and Wairahi Bay.

Smokehouse Bay in the south-west corner has become famous all over the world because it is here you can have a bath! You are invited to 'Soak and Smoke'. Soak yourself in the bath with a fire lit underneath to heat the water while your fish is being smoked in the smokehouse.

There are wharves accessible at all stages of the tide at Port Fitzroy, Whangaparapara and Shoal Bay. The Department of Conservation pontoon is available for public use. All wharves have donation boxes.

Dog owners are asked to keep their animals on a lead so they will not harm any wildlife or farm stock. Dogs are not allowed within Coopers Castle, Hirakimata, Palmers Track, Hogsback and Te Ahumata areas because here the rare black petrel nest on the ground. A dog permit is required for all dogs on Department of Conservation land.

Launching ramps

Port Fitzroy has a ramp for runabouts to land.

Recreation

Beaches

The sandy beaches are on the east coast, which is approximately 13 km from Port Fitzroy or Whangaparapara by road. The west coast beaches at Gooseberry Flat, Okupu, Bush's Beach-Kaiarara Bay are suitable for children to play on and for picnics.

Camping

There are camping grounds at the Department of Conservation headquarters in Port Fitzroy, at Harataonga, Awana, Medlands Beach and Whangaparapara for which there is a charge. Huts are available at Kaiarara and Whangaparapara with donations expected in boxes provided. The camps have toilets, barbecues and water and the huts have 24 bunks, kitchen and wood range, toilets and tank water.

Fires are a major hazard on the island and are only allowed in areas provided in huts and camping grounds with restrictions during the summer. Campers should take portable cooking equipment (gas or liquid fuel). Gas coin-operated barbecues at Bush's Beach and Department of Conservation headquarters can be used for picnics.

Walks

The Department of Conservation controls about 8000 hectares of regenerating kauri forest in the central and northern region of the island. In 1973 this was made a State Forest Recreation Area to enable public access. In 1987 restructuring of government departments saw the demise of the New Zealand Forest Service and Lands and Survey Department and the Department of Conservation inherited all Forest Service land and Lands and Survey reserves.

There are many walks in the area, varying from short walks for people of any age to routes more suited to people experienced in bush walking. The only prohibited area is Wairahi Forest Sanctuary where entry is by permit only.

From Christmas to the end of January, the Department of Conservation runs a holiday

Sailing past False Head, Great Barrier Island

programme with guided walks and activities, such as night exploring and bush survival. There are also children's sessions. Details are available from the department's headquarters or the Department of Conservation, Private Bag 8, Newton, Auckland.

A pamphlet on the walks is available and we have reproduced the information here in case you cannot obtain a copy. The Department of Conservation recommends that serious trampers use the Infomap Holidaymaker Series No 259 map. Walking times are one way.

Track 1: *Old Lady Walk, Port Fitzroy–Port Fitzroy Hill (signposted). A short, easy, alternative walk up the valley through a kauri plantation to the saddle and road. 45 minutes.*

Track 1A: *Old Lady Walk–Lookout Rock (signposted). From the signpost on Track 1, the track climbs steeply to a vantage point overlooking Port Fitzroy Harbour. 30 minutes.*

Track 2: *Fitzroy Road Saddle–Coopers Castle (signposted). Begins opposite Karaka Bay Road turn-off and ascends the southern ridge from which views of both sides of the island may be seen. Descends from summit to Murray's Camp by the Kaiarara Stream and joins with Track 6. Two hours.*

Track 2A: *Track 2 to Coopers Castle (signposted). A short climb to a promontory off Track 2 for extensive views of Okiwi Basin. Five minutes.*

Track 3: *Warren's Track (signposted). Begins at Department of Conservation headquarters at Port Fitzroy. A gently graded track which passes named trees and a kauri plantation to a waterfall. Many cold pools in the stream are deep enough for swimming. 30 minutes.*

Track 4: *Kaiarara Stream–Kiwiriki–Maungapiko (signposted). Begins at signpost for Department of Conservation road near Kaiarara Stream rising gently to junction with Track 4B then descends to Coffin's Creek (Houroaroa). Crosses* to climb steeply and follow the dividing ridge. Bears right dropping to Kiwiriki Stream which it crosses to climb a valley and central ridge to Department of Conservation road. Four hours.

Track 4A: *Track 4 to Bush's Beach (signposted). Five minutes.*

Track 4B: *'Line W' Track to Department of Conservation road (signposted). From Track 4 climb steadily to Kaiarara Plateau and Department of Conservation road. 20 minutes.*

Track 4C: *A shoreline walk to the campsite at the head of Kiwiriki Bay. 15 minutes.*

Track 4D: *Department of Conservation road to Maungapiko (signposted). Climbs steeply to promontory for view to south. 10 minutes.*

Track 5: *Kaiarara Stream to Kaiarara Plateau (signposted). Begins at signpost on Department of Conservation road near Kaiarara Stream climbing at ridge sharply to the Kaiarara Plateau. 30 minutes.*

Note: No dogs allowed on Tracks 6, 7 and 9 ascending Hirakimata.

Track 6: *Kaiarara Stream to Hirakimata (Mt Hobson) signposted. Follows Old Bridle Track past Kaiarara Hut and left of Department of Conservation road then steadily up the north-east fork of the Kaiarara Stream to the junction with Track 2. Continues upstream to the lowest kauri dam track, top fork junction and foot bridge. Crosses bridge. Climbs steeply to the top right dam. Crosses to top left dam then more steeply to Hirakimata's summit. Views of Great Barrier and offshore islands and the Hauraki Gulf. Pools in the lower Kaiarara Stream are popular with swimmers. Three hours.*

Track 6A: *Track 6 to Selwyns (signposted). Climbs ridge between northern forks of the Kaiarara Stream through pole kauri and hardwood. 30 minutes.*

Track 6B: *Track 6 to Track 8 Link (signposted). Begins on Track 6, 74 m above Track 6A junction, following the gently graded southern fork of the Kaiarara Stream to Track 8. 30 minutes.*

Track 7: *Palmers Track to Hirakimata (signposted). Begins on summit of Fitzroy–Harataonga Road, climbing through Windy Canyon to central ridge. Views either side of Okiwi and Kaitoke. Follows ridge and climbs steeply to Hirakimata's summit through unlogged mature subalpine forest. There is no fresh water near the track. Three hours.*

Old kauri dam, Great Barrier Island

Track 8: *Department of Conservation road to South Fork, Kaiarara Stream—Mt Heale—Hirakimata (signposted). Begins on Department of Conservation road approximately 1 km south of Kaiarara Hut. Descends to Kaiarara Stream, crosses twice and follows Old Bridle Track before crossing again and climbing central ridge steadily before levelling out at junction of Track 8B. Around Mt Heale and steep ascent to Hirakimata. Three hours.*

Track 8A: *Track 8 to Kauri Dam. Drops rapidly from Track 8 to southern fork of Kaitoke Stream and kauri dam. 15 minutes.*

Track 8B: *Track 8 to Track 10. Drops rapidly from Track 8 below Mt Heale to Track 10 at Peach Tree hot spring (old Kauri Timber Company campsite). One hour.*

The smokehouse, Great Barrier Island

Track 9: *Coffins Creek—Kiwiriki Stream—Department of Conservation road. Steady rise from road following telephone line from Coffins Creek to high ridge. Descends to Kiwiriki Stream and rises again to Department of Conservation road. 45 minutes.*

Track 9A: *Loop track to kauri trees (signposted). From Track 9 north of Kiwiriki*

Stream an easy walk to kauri tree No. 1. Back track to signpost then descend to kauri tree No. 2, the largest kauri tree on the island. Short ascent back to Track 9.

Track 10: *This follows an old Kauri Timber Company tramline from Fitzroy via Harataonga Road to Whangaparapara Harbour (signposted). From Fitzroy, Harataonga Road descends steadily then abruptly to Awana Stream and waterfall. A steep ascent to plateau, Perrys Hill and Track 10A junction before dropping to Kaitoke Creek. The track follows and crosses the creek at a gradual grade above and around the Kaitoke Swamp. It climbs again and descends to Kaitoke Creek No. 2 then up to the Department of Conservation road. Walk south along road for 250 m then turn right on tramline down over Whangaparapara Creek to Whangaparapara Hut. Track levels out following creek to open grassland and harbour. Six hours.*

Track 10A: *Awana Road to Track 10. From Awana Road concrete bridge turn north-west on the four-wheel-drive track up the ridge to the junction with Track 10. One hour.*

Track 10B: *Whangaparapara Hut to Department of Conservation road (shorter route). Opposite Whangaparapara track crosses stream to climb central ridge around eucalyptus grove to Department of Conservation road. An alternative shorter route from hut to Kaitoke via the stamping battery. 30 minutes.*

Track 11: *Whangaparapara Road to Hot Springs (signposted). Right turn from the road to Whangaparapara follows a level track above the Kaitoke Swamp, which must be crossed occasionally, to sulphurous hot springs. A small pool for bathing is dammed at a fork in the Kaitoke Creek. There is a picnic area, rubbish pit and toilet. Be careful, the water may be very hot. One hour.*

Track 12: *Pack Track. Whangaparapara Hut–Wairahi Stream–Department of Conservation road (shorter route). Above Whangaparapara Hut on Track 10 cross the foot-bridge and take the left turn at the signpost on telephone track, up the ridge and down to Wairahi Stream. Climb steeply to Department of Conservation road. This is a shorter route between Kaiarara and Whangaparapara Huts. 45 minutes.*

Track 13: *Witheys Track. Links with Tracks 10 and 12. A roundabout walk from Whangaparapara on Track 10 to signpost. Then climbs ridge on left steadily before dropping to Wairahi Stream and following it up to junction with Track 12. 75 minutes.*

Track 14: *Mt Whangaparapara. From Whangaparapara cross stile and climb track to left. A steady climb to summit with views of Whangaparapara Harbour and surrounds. You have to go back the same way as the track continues into Wairahi Sanctuary and an entry permit is required for this area. 75 minutes.*

Track 15: *Whangaparapara to Mangati Bay. Cross foot-bridge from Whangaparapara, south through camping area to climb steeply to ridge top. Descend and climb again before descending to the site of Kauri Timber Company's sawmill.*

Above Smokehouse Bay

Cross site, turn right at signpost and climb again then descend to Mangati Bay. Return back along the same track. One hour.

Track 16: *Bridle Track. An alternative route between the Department of Conservation headquarters and Port Fitzroy store and post office. An easy grade passing through indigenous and exotic forest. 15 minutes.*

Track 17 *Te Ahumuta. From Whangaparapara Saddle the track follows an old mining road leading south-east. A gradual climb to signposted junction then rapid ascent following rehabilitated mining road to Te Ahumata trig. Excellent views of Kaitoke to the east and Hauraki Gulf to the west. 30 minutes.*

Warning

During recent years some people have seen fit to celebrate New Year's Eve by letting off flares at midnight. Not only is this illegal but it has caused fires, putting the safety of people and property at risk and causing much needless work for those who have fought the fire with limited resources.

The Department of Conservation is carrying out an education programme and patrolling the beaches and camping grounds during the Christmas/New Year period to advise that flares are dangerous and they will take legal action against anyone found lighting flares.

The Marlborough–Nelson area

The Marlborough Sounds, in the north-east of the South Island, are 500 sq km of bays and waterways sheltered by rugged, often bush-covered hills situated at the top end of the South Island of New Zealand. Much of the Sounds is part of the Marlborough Sounds Maritime Park and has been classified into various uses such as camping, picnicking and walking.

Landing is not allowed on the island reserves of Titi Island, Chetwode Islands or the Brothers unless a permit is obtained from the Department of Conservation. Maud Island may only be visited by arrangement with the Wildlife Service. All these islands are protected because of their scientific value and landing on them is generally restricted to naturalists or others with a special interest in wildlife.

Camping is in designated areas and not permitted on foreshore reserve (20 m inland from mean high water mark) fronting privately owned residences, nature, historic or scientific reserves, or in picnic areas.

No open fires are allowed so barbecues are provided by the Park. You can also use your own barbecue or thermette. It is suggested that driftwood be used where at all possible.

Domestic animals are not allowed in the Park.

The area has much to offer boaties, but be aware that it can be squally at times. Because of the steep sides and indented coastline the wind sometimes comes over the cliffs unexpectedly. However, because of the large number of sheltered bays it is possible to find a suitable anchorage in any wind.

Captain Cook was so taken with the beauty of the area that he visited it on five separate occasions to careen his ships and restore the health of his crew. In 1770 he named Queen Charlotte Sound after the Queen of England, the wife of King George III. At one time the town of Picton, which lies at the head of Queen Charlotte Sound, was suggested for the capital of New Zealand as it lay in the centre of the country and had a good deep water port. However, the idea was later dropped. It is named after Sir Thomas Picton, a general who never lost a battle.

Picton and Havelock, at the head of Pelorus Sound, are the main centres for the Sounds. Picton is the terminal for the Cook Strait ferries which link the North and South Islands of New Zealand. Watch out for the wash from the ferries when using Tory Channel and Queen Charlotte Sound and always give way to the ferries as commercial shipping has right of way.

There are roads out to many parts of the Sounds, so you can arrange to meet friends. There are also several tourist resorts out in the bays, many of which allow boaties to use their facilities and also offer meals.

Several commercial mail and ferry services cover the area and it is possible to arrange for supplies to be delivered to your boat.

To the west of the Marlborough Sounds is th·

picturesque Tasman Bay. On one side of the Bay is Nelson, the largest city of the region, while on the other side is the Abel Tasman National Park.

Nelson is the geographical centre of New Zealand and is named after the famous naval hero Horatio Nelson. Many of the streets have names associated with him, for example Trafalgar Street, Collingwood Street and Hardy Street.

It is a large town with all manner of services for the boatie and places of interest for the crew to visit. It has one of the highest sunshine ratings in the country.

The National Park is named after Abel Tasman, the Dutch explorer who visited the area in 1642. The French explorer d'Urville visited nearly two centuries later in 1827 on the *Astrolabe* and spent a week in the Astrolabe roadstead near Marahau surveying and collecting plants.

In 1841 three ships of the New Zealand Company began explorations for the settlement of the area and eventually there were farmers, boat builders, timber millers and quarrymen living and working along the coast. However, there is very little sign of these activities today. The land was set aside as a park in 1942 to commemorate the tricentenary of Abel Tasman's visit.

Picton

Chart No: 615 Marlborough Sounds
Chart No: 6153 Queen Charlotte
Sound, Picton Harbour, Picton
Wharves

Map No: Infomap Holidaymaker 301
– Marlborough Sounds
Navigation Information: *Cruising Guide:*
Cape Palliser to Marlborough Sounds and
Tasman Bay by Keith Murray and
Ralph von Kohorn

Facilities

Picton township is on the harbour so it is not far to walk to any of the facilities. There are street lights at night.

 FUEL fuel berth on west side of harbour for petrol, diesel and two-stroke.

 GAS/KEROSENE at garage.

 WATER on wharf.

 STORES Picton has all the usual shops and services of an average town such as supermarket, clothing stores, banks, post office, library, doctors, dentist, chandlery and boat services, restaurants and take-aways. There is also a shop in the ferry terminal.

 TOILETS on wharf; foreshore below Memorial Steps; Plunket Rooms, Wellington Street; Red Cross Rooms, Auckland Street.

 SHOWERS Harbour Board showers, coin operated.

 LAUNDRY Harbour Board laundry with drier, coin operated.

 HARBOUR-MASTER the services for visiting boaties are organised by the Marlborough Harbour Board Small Craft Supervisor. His office is on the Town Wharf.

 TELEPHONE at post office, corner Wellington St and London Quay, and in ferry terminal.

 POLICE station at top end of High Street; telephone 36-439.

 REPAIRS there are four slipways in Picton and three at Waikawa, not far from Picton. Hardstand area is available to rent from the Marlborough Harbour Board if required.

 WEATHER INFORMATION on local radio: Radio Marlborough, 2ZE 1539kh.

 TRANSPORT there are bus services to other parts of the country; train to Christchurch; ferry to Wellington; and minibus services which include mail delivery and make an interesting way to see the country.

Picton

Anchorage

Picton is sheltered from east through south to north-west, but north to north-east winds blow straight in.

The Marlborough Harbour Board has several berths for visitors. East of the ferry terminal are three jetties with space for 30 boats. There are short-term berths in front of the town wharf and room for launches under the coat-hanger bridge. They will always find room for a visitor and in summer when there is great demand they usually put a barge in the long-arm and tie boats up to it. There are also seven swing moorings just around from the ferry terminal and seven in Shakespeare Bay.

On arrival in the port it is probably best to tie up to one of the visitors' berths at the town wharf and then contact the small craft supervisor in his office on the wharf. Boats are allowed to stay for a short time at the wharf to get stores on board.

Charges – When a boat arrives in Picton the skipper is sold a harbour dues sticker which gives the first 12 hours' berthage free on each visit to Picton plus use of Harbour Board swing moorings and jetties in the Sounds. This costs $21.45 per annum and helps towards the cost of navigational aids in the Sounds. After the initial 12 hours the cost is on a per day basis – at time of writing $5.50 per day for a jetty, $2.20 per day for a swing mooring.

Launching ramps

South of ferry terminal, Picton Marina, off Waikawa Road, Waikawa Marina via Beach Road. Marlborough Harbour Board makes a charge for the use of its ramps.

Recreation

Picton is a pleasant little town with plenty of activity and it is worth spending some time there. The information centre in Auckland Street is full of ideas and the staff are most helpful.

The township slopes down to the harbour and is dominated by the sight of ships and water. It is fun to sit on the foreshore and watch the activity including the Cook Strait ferries. They make an impressive sight as they steam down Queen Charlotte Sound – there are several sailings each day.

Children's activities

For children there is a playground on the foreshore full of equipment such as swings, slides and see-saws, and nearby are bumper boats, mini-motor bikes and mini-golf. During the holiday season the Model Engineers' Club operates train rides.

Museum

The Smith Memorial Museum situated on the foreshore is open seven days a week from 10 a.m. to 4 p.m. It contains relics of the whaling industry and the sailing ship Edwin Fox, and there is a Maori section and an old Picton section. Admission is adults $1 and children 50c or a family ticket for $2.50.

Library

In Upper High Street. Opening hours Monday to Friday 10 a.m. to 12.30 p.m. and 1.30 p.m. to 4.30 p.m. Also Friday evenings 7 p.m. to 8.30 p.m.

Walks

There are several walks around the foreshore. Bob's Bay along the eastern side is about one kilometre each way. This is a popular swimming and water-skiing spot and there are also toilets and barbecues.

Victoria Domain off Waikawa Road (on the left going away from town) has several bush walks and spectacular views.

The Tirohanga Walk also offers spectacular views. Beginning at Newgate Street off Waikawa Road (on the right going away from town) it winds up the hill above the town. It takes about an hour to climb and there is a look-out area at the top giving a wonderful view of Picton below and the Sounds stretching out beyond.

Essons Valley is an easy 90-minute-return walk from Garden Terrace at the back of the town through delightful native bush to the borough's catchment dams.

Going in the opposite direction from the town is Queen Charlotte Drive, which has panoramic views of Picton and the Sounds. Either walk along the road or take the track from the cement silos (Waitohi Wharf) near the ferry terminal.

Sports

Squash courts – Visitors can play by obtaining key from Picton Garden Centre, High Street.

Tennis – public courts, Memorial Park, Surrey Street.

Bowls – Picton Bowling Club, corner Kent Street and Broadway.

Golf – Picton Golf Club, Koromiko, about six kilometres from town on State Highway 1.

Swimming – community pool, Queen Charlotte College.

Marlborough Cruising Club

The clubhouse is the old boat Echo on the foreshore at Shelley Beach. It is open 4.40 p.m. to 9 p.m. on Sundays. Postal address, PO Box 99, Picton.

Queen Charlotte Sound

Besides the Marlborough Harbour Board's moorings in the Sounds there are yacht club moorings for use by members. These are owned by Mana Cruising Club, PO Box 2506, Wellington; Waikawa Boating Club, PO Box 426, Blenheim; and Pelorus Boating Club, PO Box 1, Havelock. Enquiries about membership and the use of these moorings should be made to them.

Grove Arm

Leaving Picton the Grove Arm is to port and has some good sandy beaches and bays with facilities. It usually has less strength of wind and has easy access from Picton so it is a good first stop for newcomers to the Sounds. The prevailing wind is north to north-west.

Governors Bay

This is an idyllic picnic spot accessible both from the water and road, sheltered from the south-west to west. Runabouts can drive up on to the beach. Access from the road is via a short walking track down the cliff. There are toilets but no other facilities.

Ngakuta Bay

Keep hard to port when entering as the starboard (south-east) side dries at low tide. Picnic area, toilets, dairy, morning and afternoon teas, boat launching ramp. Road access. No fuel.

Momorangi Bay

There are many facilities for boaties, including wharf with fuel and water, launching ramp, camping ground with facilities, store, public toilets and telephone. Road access. Sheltered from the south but open to west to north-west.

Anakiwa Walk

Running from Anakiwa, home of the Outward Bound School, at the head of the Grove Arm to Portage on Kenepuru Sound, this walk takes six and a half hours and is in two sections:
- Anakiwa to Mistletoe Bay – three and a half hours
- Mistletoe Bay to Portage – three hours.

There is road access at Anakiwa and Portage and restricted access to Mistletoe Bay. From Anakiwa the track follows the coast to above Bottle Bay, accessible by sea only. It then climbs to approximately 200 m above sea-level before traversing the saddle behind Mistletoe Bay. The track continues along the main ridge separating Kenepuru and Queen Charlotte Sound to Portage. There are good views of both sounds and it is a good place to get an overview of the sunken valleys which make up the sounds. There are camping areas at Davies Bay (one hour from Anakiwa) and Cowshed Bay (300 m west of Portage).

Inner Queen Charlotte Sound

The prevailing wind is north-west to north. Yachts should stay in the middle of the sound to avoid the calm patches between each bay and the gusts across the mouth. The tidal flow is half to one knot.

Onahau Bay

There are some good anchorages in this bay plus two public jetties and moorings. At the head of the bay is Mistletoe Bay recreation reserve. There is a small grassed picnic area surrounded by dense stands of regenerating bush. Access is by sea or via the Kenepuru Road (turn off just before Te Mahia). Public toilets. There is accommodation for groups

Sailing by the Picton ferry

involved in outdoor education. Contact the Department of Conservation, PO Box 445, Blenheim, for further details.

Double Cove

Fishing is prohibited in this bay and the fish are so tame they will eat bread out of your hand. This is a fun place for children to visit.

Torea Bay

This bay is just across the saddle from Portage on Kenepuru Sound. It has Marlborough Harbour Board moorings and a wharf for loading and unloading passengers. A short walk over the saddle takes you to Portage where there is a licensed tourist resort with a shop.

Kumutoto Bay

Public jetty. Camping area. Public toilets. Picnic area. Separate area for water-skiing.

Bay of Many Coves

Cockle Cove has a good anchorage plus mooring. East Bay has a nice beach. There is an abundance of scallops in the bay for divers. Facilities include petrol and diesel, provisions and a holiday resort which offers moderately priced cabins, some with own toilet and shower. The Gem Resort is set in 60 hectares, much of it native bush with birds such as fantails, bellbirds, wekas and wood-pigeons. Fish in the bay include blue cod, terakihi, gurnard, snapper and kahawai. No road access.

Endeavour Inlet

Provisions, moorings and holiday resort at Punga Cove. Furneaux Lodge on the starboard side of the northern inlet has water, fuel, stores and dive air. The lodge was built nearly a century ago in the style of a French colonial homestead and named after Captain Furneaux of the sailing ship *Adventurer* who landed nearby in 1784 for a meeting with Captain Cook. At the head of the inlet is a privately owned camp, the Endeavour Inlet Holiday Camp. Safe swimming, fishing and bush walks.

Endeavour Walk

There is a walk from Endeavour Inlet to Ship Cove through areas steeped in early European New Zealand history. It is in three sections as follows:
● Camp Bay to Furneaux Lodge – four hours
● Furneaux Lodge to Resolution Bay – three hours
● Resolution Bay to Ship Cove – two hours.

The track starts at the Kenepuru Saddle immediately after Camp Bay and after descending into the Bay follows the coast around the head of Endeavour Inlet. From the east coast of Endeavour Inlet the track climbs to a saddle before descending into Resolution Bay. The final section to Ship Cove is through some excellent examples of native forest and includes a look-out on the main ridge which provides spectacular views of Cook Strait and the outer Queen Charlotte Sound. Private camping areas are available at the head of Endeavour Inlet and Resolution Bay and a public camping area at Camp Bay and at the Pines. There is a picnic site at Ship Cove, but no camping is allowed.

If some of the crew want to do the walk one way the rest could take the boat and meet them either at Ship Cove or Resolution Bay.

Resolution Bay

Open to south-east to south but otherwise good shelter. There is a holiday resort and stores. Access by sea and track only. The bay was named after the *Resolution* in which Captain Cook made his second visit to New Zealand in 1773–74 and his third in 1777.

Ship Cove

The end of the walk from Camp Bay, Ship Cove, has a public jetty and moorings, a picnic area surrounded by native bush, safe sandy beaches, a stream and toilets. Holding is poor where the swift-flowing river runs into the Bay between the wharf and monument. Access is by sea and track only.

A typical private wharf, Marlborough Sounds

Motuara Island

Marlborough Sounds Maritime Park wharf at centre of the western side of the island with 4 m of water at low water springs. Short walk to the look-out and views of Cook Strait and Queen Charlotte Sound. In 1770 Captain Cook raised the Union Jack, taking formal possession of the island and adjacent lands in the name of the king and naming the area Queen Charlotte Sound after the queen.

Cape Jackson

If you are going round the Cape to Pelorus Sound try to go with the tide as it can be rough.

Tory Channel

This is the route of the Cook Strait ferries. There are several sailings each day between Wellington and Picton and the ferries have right of way over other boats. Be careful of the wash. There is a tidal stream of up to seven knots at the entrance of the channel and four knots elsewhere.

Hitaua Bay, which has a club mooring, offers some shelter from the ferry wash. Castaways Resort at Te Pangu offers evening meals by arrangement, showers and stores plus self-contained units for those needing accommodation. No road access.

On Arapawa Island, East Bay Homestay, Onauku Station offers accommodation for fishing and diving parties. Moorings are available.

Havelock

Facilities

 FUEL at wharf, tokens from Shell garage 200 m away.

 GAS BOTTLES refilled at garage.

 WATER at main wharf.

 STORES all requirements are available in the small shopping centre in the main street. These include a seven-day supermarket which will also send supplies out on the mail boat, chandlery and hardware shop, marine engineer, restaurant and take-aways, and a pottery shop which has some interesting and unusual pieces.

 TOILETS in marina.

 SHOWERS/LAUNDRY at Pelorus Boating Club for members' use only. However, facilities may be available on application to the Secretary, PO Box 1, Havelock. The camping ground close to the marina allows visiting boaties to use their laundry and showers.

 HARBOUR-MASTER Ken Paget. Available 7 a.m. to 6 p.m. weekdays, 8 a.m. to 5 p.m. weekends. After hours telephone 42-140. Mr Paget is also the Search and Rescue co-ordinator.

 TELEPHONE on main wharf, available 24 hours.

 POLICE station is opposite the pub.

 REPAIRS Harbour Board grid and haul-out area. Chandlery and various services such as outboard repairs and marine engineering in the township.

 POSTAL post office is in main street. No banks.

 MARINE RADIO Havelock Association Radio VHF 63 and 16, SSB 2045.

 DIVE AIR The Dive Shop, Water St.

 TRANSPORT Havelock is on the main road between Picton and Nelson. There are bus services each way. Water transport is available out to the Sounds and the mail boat takes passengers. A trip on the mail boat is a good way to see the life of the Sounds. There are different routes during the week. The trips are long and possibly not suitable for very young children who could become bored or elderly people who would become uncomfortable.

  ACCOMMODATION motel, motor camp and youth hostel. The youth hostel is an old school (one of its former pupils was Lord Ernest Rutherford, who was the first person to split the atom).

Havelock, a small fishing town, is the main supply area at the head of Pelorus Sound with all facilities required by boaties. The Marlborough Harbour Board will find visitors a berth in the marina and there is safe parking for cars and trailers. The harbour-master is very helpful and has a pamphlet giving details of the approaches to Havelock.

Yachts drawing more than a metre should

approach Havelock two hours each side of high water and preferably on an incoming tide. Minimum depth of water in Havelock Harbour is approximately two metres.

The channel is very narrow in places and yachts should use their motors from Black Point as there is no room to manoeuvre. The current runs at up to three knots close to the shore from Havelock to Black Point. In addition there is a 1.1 m difference in tide from Nelson on spring tides.

Eighty percent of the work-force of Havelock is employed in the mussel trade and the mussel barges are a feature of the Sound. Please give way as they are restricted by draught and time commitments.

Other recommendations from the Harbour Board are as follows:

● Do not attempt to head directly from number 2 beacon to number 5 beacon, and to be safe your vessel should be within 50 metres adjacent to Shag Point before approaching number 5 beacon.

● Shoal area marked as SSSS on diagram adjacent to number 7 beacon encroaches across part of the channel and a slightly western approach as indicated is advised when approaching number 7 beacon.

● PVC poles from number 7 beacon to the harbour entrance mark one side of the channel.

● There is a speed restriction of five knots in the area of Cullens Point.

Anchorage

There are no berths specifically set aside for visitors but the harbour-master will allocate a berth. There is usually room for up to 20 visiting boats. To arrange a visitors' berth tie up to the main wharf and go to the harbour-master's office on the wharf. Alternatively anchor in the anchorage at the end of the marina. Take care to keep clear of the launching ramp.

An item of interest in the marina area is one of the lifeboats from the Russian cruise ship *Mikhail Lermontov*, which sank in Port Gore between Queen Charlotte and Pelorus Sounds. The liner itself is now a popular diving place.

Launching ramp

There is a charge for using the launching ramp. Pay at the harbour-master's office. It is $4 per day including parking. Regular users can buy a monthly launching ticket. Secure car and trailer parking is available at $5 per day, $45 per fortnight or $75 per month. Each parking space will take three vehicles.

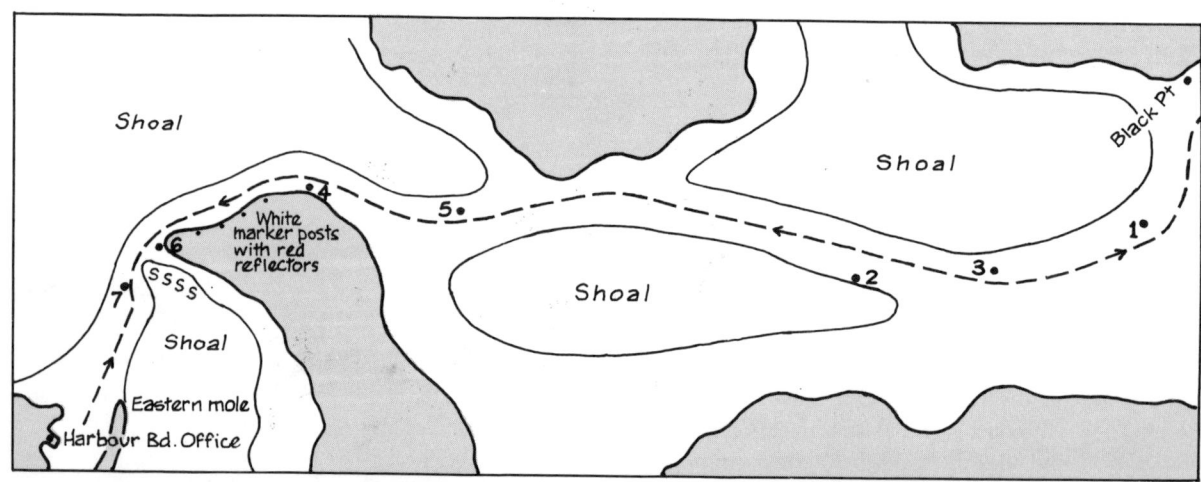

Name	No	Structure	Light	Range
Black Point		White pile beacon	Flash White 5 secs	5 miles
Moutapu	1	White & Green pile beacon	Flash Green 3 secs	3 miles
Hoods Bay	2	White & Red pile beacon	Flash Red 3 secs	3 miles
	3	White & Green pile beacon	Flash Green 3 secs	3 miles
Shag Point		White beacon on shore	Flash White 3 secs	3 miles
	5	White & Green pile beacon	Flash Green 5 secs	2 miles
Pull 'N' Be Damned	4	White beacon on shore	Flash Red 3 secs	1 mile
Cullen Point		White beacon on shore	Flash White 3 secs	3 miles
	7	White and Green pile beacon	Flash Green 3 secs	1 mile
Eastern Mole		White beacon on shore	Flash Red 3 secs	1 miles

Information kindly supplied by the Marlborough Harbour Board, Havelock.

Recreation

Glow-worms

Most people have heard of the Waitomo Glow-worm Caves but did you know Havelock has glow-worms?

You will find them by walking up behind the War Memorial Gardens after dark – take a torch. The first glow-worms can be seen within a few minutes' walk past the fire station and back entrance to the Garden Motels. As you move up the track they are mainly on the right-hand side suspended from the bank. Beyond the reservoir to where the narrow track meets the creek you will find yourself surrounded by myriads of blue, starry lights.

Takorika walkway

A continuation of the glow-worm walk in daylight becomes a one-hour walk along a loop track taking in some attractive stream beds, small waterfalls and picturesque views. Watch for bellbirds, tuis and fantails in the bush.

For the more energetic this can become a four-hour walk. Follow the creek up to a wide fire-break and on to Takorika summit (720 m). This gives good views of the township and Sounds. An alternative route down, although steep in parts, is the fire-break which comes out about one kilometre north of the township. Take a snack and drink, and wear good shoes.

Boat trips

If you want to take a busman's holiday and let someone else worry about navigation around the Sounds while you enjoy the scenery there are several boat trips for sightseeing or fishing. They are advertised around the town and marina, or enquire at the travel office in the main street. Transport to the guest houses in the Sounds is also available.

The mail-boat trip is interesting because it gives an insight into the lives of people in isolated areas of the Sounds. In some places there are jetties where the locals come down to meet the boat; in other bays the locals row out in dinghies to collect their mail and supplies. The mail-boat is their link with the outside world as there are no roads to many of the homesteads.

Morning and afternoon teas are provided on the mail-boat trip, but take your own lunch and some warm clothing. It is a long day and what can start out as a beautiful sunny morning can turn into quite a chilly afternoon, especially on the route out to the entrance where the Sounds meet Cook Strait.

Sports

Bowls – Havelock Bowling Club welcomes visitors. The club is open Tuesday and Thursday evenings and weekends.

Tennis – Public tennis courts behind the general store are available to visitors. Racquets can be hired from the Garden Motels, telephone 42-387.

Pelorus Sound

Pelorus Sound is larger and more rugged than Queen Charlotte Sound and includes several islands and many areas inaccessible by road. For trailer boats it is only a short journey by road from Picton, but larger boats will have to go out into Cook Strait around Cape Jackson and enter the Sound either via Guards Bay, Allen Strait and Forsyth Bay or via the West Entry near Bulwer and Port Ligar.

When entering or leaving Havelock keep in mind the warnings from the Harbour Board and follow its diagram in order to negotiate the channel safely.

Pipi Beach

The first picnic stop from Havelock is Pipi Beach on the port-hand side. This has a public toilet but no other facilities and no road access. It is not an overnight anchorage, just a picnic stop and somewhere for the children to stretch their legs.

Nydia Walkway

Nydia Bay is the half-way point of the Nydia Walkway, which runs from Kaiuma opposite Havelock to Duncan Bay on Tennyson Inlet. There is vehicle access to either end of the track but boaties may like to do part of the track starting at Nydia Bay or Duncan Bay.

Those without boats can make arrangements to be dropped off or collected by the mail-boat from Havelock. Enquire at the travel office in Havelock's main street.

The track was completed in 1979 and passes over

A meeting at sea

bridle paths constructed as long ago as 1900. It is part of the New Zealand Walkways system and suitable for the reasonably fit. Times are as follows:

- Kaiuma to Nydia Bay – five and a half hours.
- Nydia Bay to Ngawhakawhiti Bay – four hours.
- Ngawhakawhiti Bay to Duncan Bay – 1 hour.

There are campsites at Nydia Bay and Ngawhaka-whiti. Toilets are provided but you must take your own cooking facilities. There is space for six small tents at each site. No domestic animals are allowed and you are asked to take away your rubbish.

Starting at Kaiuma the first half hour's walk along the Kaiuma Valley passes through farm land. From the head of the valley the track climbs through native forest to the Kaiuma Saddle before dropping down into Nydia Bay. The track then follows the western coast of Nydia Bay and on the way to Duncan Bay passes through some fine stands of native beech forest.

Because of the different terrain there is variety in flora and fauna. Introduced species of birds frequent the farm land while the native birds are found in the bush. During the last glaciation the Sounds remained ice-free, acting as a sanctuary for many organisms. As a result, native trees such as the nikau palm and titoki, uncommon elsewhere in the South Island, are found throughout the Pelorus area.

It is suggested that you take some fly repellant with you – in every paradise there is a flaw!

Nydia Bay was originally known by Maori inhabitants as Opouri and a pa existed on its northern side. The name Opouri means 'place of sadness'. According to legend a hapu – part of a tribe – was preparing to migrate from the North Island to the Sounds. The leader of the hapu killed a young boy as an offering to Tangaroa, god of the sea, to ensure a safe journey. When the boy's father found out what had happened he sought utu (revenge). He and the remaining men of the tribe set off for Pelorus Sound where they slaughtered their treacherous relatives.

Facilities for today's visitors to Nydia Bay include the campsite, public toilet, picnic area and jetty. There is also a public lodge with bunk accommodation, kitchen facilities and hot showers. Enquiries to Department of Conservation, PO Box 161, Picton.

Jacobs Bay

Jetty, picnic area, camping and toilets on the port-side going towards the open sea. This is a good place for children to have a play and has no road access. There is a short walk (30 minutes) to Dillon Bell Point.

Fairy Bay

Similar to Jacobs Bay but no jetty.

North-west Bay

A good anchorage in all but south-easterly. If wind does come from south-east, change to bay opposite for shelter.

Te Rawa

Te Rawa is at the end of the peninsula which separates Pelorus Sound and Tennyson Inlet. Petrol, diesel and provisions are available and there is tourist accommodation at the Te Rawa Boatel. Fresh milk and meat may be available from the farm next door. No road access.

There are boat club moorings in the bay for use by members of the appropriate clubs.

Maud Island

Maud Island is a bird sanctuary and no landing is allowed unless special permission is obtained from the Wildlife Service.

Tennyson Inlet

This is a beautiful area with trees down to the water's edge. It has good anchorage but no beaches. There is road access for trailer boats, with launching ramps at Tuna Bay, Penzance Bay and Duncan Bay. Tuna Bay has fuel and water and club moorings.

Penzance Bay is a popular spot and a regatta is held at New Year. There are club moorings, a jetty, picnic area and toilets. There are two walks from Penzance Bay to Elaine Bay; one via the Archer Track which takes three hours and the other via the Hard Beech Track which takes three and a half hours. As with other walks from bay to bay, some of the crew may like to walk while others take the boat to meet them.

Penzance Bay is at the end of one road and Elaine Bay at the end of another. They are joined only by the track. Elaine Bay has a camping area, picnic spot, toilets and jetty.

Bulwer

Bulwer is at the entrance to Pelorus Sound and is the first fuelling and provisioning point if you have made the trip from Wellington. It has very deep water (30–40 m). There are club moorings and guest accommodation. It is accessible by road.

Admiralty Bay

Admiralty Bay, on the other side of the peninsula from Bulwer, has some quite good anchorages and fuel and provisions are available at French Pass.

Outer Sounds

Titirangi in Guards Bay provides a good first anchorage after crossing Cook Strait, provided the wind is not from the north. There are no shops or fuel but there is a campsite with cold showers and toilets, picnic area, sandy beach and accommodation. It is accessible by road but the road is steep and unsuitable for cars towing loads. There is a club mooring.

Beware of the strong current through Allen Strait which runs between Forsyth Island and the mainland. Another danger area is French Pass between D'Urville Island and the mainland. The current runs through the pass at up to eight knots and it is very narrow. Use the period of slack water if at all possible.

French Pass has one of the few sandy beaches in the Sounds as well as a camping area, toilets, cold showers, jetty, boat ramp and a short walking track. There are club moorings, fuel and provisions. It is accessible by road.

D'Urville Island

D'Urville Island is the second largest offshore island in New Zealand. On the way to the island from Pelorus Sound you pass the Chetwode Islands, which are a bird sanctuary. There is shelter from a westerly wind if necessary, but beware of rocks and do not land. Trio Islands are also a bird sanctuary and home to the tuatara, New Zealand's prehistoric reptile, but landing is not allowed.

Nearby are the Rangitoto Islands, not to be confused with the volcanic cone that can be seen from virtually any part of Auckland and as much a part of that city as the harbour bridge.

Stephens Island is at the top end of D'Urville and the passage between the two has a strong current. However, there is good fishing, mainly blue cod, in this area.

First bay on the west side of D'Urville is Port Hardy. The water is deep and there are many good anchoring bays. It is bordered by private land and reserves. There are camping and picnicking areas at Philante Cove and South Arm but no facilities. It is very peaceful in Port Hardy except in north-west conditions which can be quite hazardous. Shellfish, such as mussels, pipi and paua, are to be found and divers will find crayfish.

The next bay going down the west coast is Greville Harbour but be careful of the strong current round Nile Head. The coastline is very rugged with high bluffs. A boulder bank at the entrance to Greville Harbour is clearly marked with painted poles. Caution is needed entering and leaving and it is best to go with the tide. Water is available from a hose at the eastern arm of the harbour. There is a camping and picnicking area but no facilities.

Catherine Cove, on the east coast, is a popular anchorage but can be very windy. There is an easy walking track.

For boats returning to Nelson from the Sounds there are no anchorages until Croiselles Harbour. Care is needed as reefs extend off the islands around the entrance. Recommended entry is from the south side of the islands as the north entrance is very shallow. There are some good anchorages but take care around mussel rafts.

Kenepuru Sound

Kenepuru Sound runs off Pelorus to the east. This does have road access and is quite commercialised with several tourist facilities.

It is about one hour from Havelock to the entrance to this Sound, which has several good anchorages and beaches. There is shelter on either side of the Sound and the tourist resorts offer various facilities, including licensed restaurants, so find something special to celebrate while you are on holiday here. Because it is accessible by road, you can arrange to meet friends.

There are camping areas at Cowshed Bay, Picnic Bay, Schoolhouse Bay, Wander Bay and Ferndale Bay with access by sea or road.

Te Mahia Bay

Te Mahia Bay has a motel and caravan park set in a bay with a beautiful beach surrounded by native bush. It has boat-launching facilities and moorings, and a well-stocked shop.

Tourist facilities

The Portage Hotel is possibly the best known of the tourist facilities in this area. Last century a farmhouse at the foot of the hill was converted to a guest-house

A weekend cruise

and known as the Portage. It was so called because it was the spot where first the Maori and later Europeans carried their boats over the low saddle which separates Kenepuru and Queen Charlotte Sounds. Today the Portage has become a major hotel with a licensed restaurant, but it retains its links with the past. The restaurant's rich wood panelling is part of the original guest-house. There is a public jetty and petrol and diesel are available.

On the opposite shore are Raetihi Lodge and St Omer House. Raetihi Lodge is a guest-house with a licensed restaurant. St Omer House has accommodation in rooms, cabins and tent sites. It also has a shop.

Nelson

Chart No: 614 Tasman Bay
Chart No: 6142 Nelson Roads,
Port Nelson

Map No: Infomap 260 Series N27/027

Facilities

 FUEL   McCully Service Centre, Vickerman Street.

 GAS BOTTLES   McCully Service Centre, Vickerman Street; Nelgas, 163 Haven Road.

 WATER   at landing barge in boat harbour.

 STORES   there are several businesses in Vickerman Street within the harbour area which have all the services likely to be required such as outboard service, chandlery, sail maker, slipway, electrical repairs, canvas repairs, marine engineer. A limited range of foodstuffs is available in the harbour area at a lunch bar and the garages. However, it is only a short distance to the main township where there is a full range of stores of food (including a good health food store), clothing, books, gifts, sports goods.
Banks — several in town centre.

 RUBBISH DISPOSAL   bins provided in harbour area.

 TOILETS/SHOWERS   adjacent to launching ramp and careening grid. Shower keys are available from the small craft supervisor $10 deposit. The showers take 20 cent coins to operate.

 HARBOUR-MASTER   Capt. B.J. Westbrooke; telephone Nelson 82-099.

 TELEPHONE   at post office, corner Halifax and Trafalgar Streets.

 POLICE   Nelson 88-309.

 FIRST AID   Nelson Hospital, Waimea Road, entrance Kawai Street; telephone Nelson 88-299. Hospital can also give name of rostered duty doctor.

 REPAIRS   careening grid on the north-west corner of the old boat harbour outside the toilet/shower block. No charge. Book with small-craft supervisor at the Harbour Board office.

 POSTAL   post office on corner Halifax and Trafalgar Streets, diagonally opposite information centre.

 LOCAL RADIO   Radio Nelson 1341Khz. Marine conditions broadcast hourly after news.

 WEATHER FORECAST   Nelson Meteorological Office; telephone 729-920.

 TIDAL RANGE   3.97 metres.

 EATING OUT   there is a wide range of restaurants for all tastes and budgets plus take-away bars if you want to eat on board but do not want to cook.

 ACCOMMODATION   full details at Public Relations Office, corner Halifax and Trafalgar Streets; telephone Nelson 82-304. The Youth Hostel is in Weka Street, not far from the town centre.

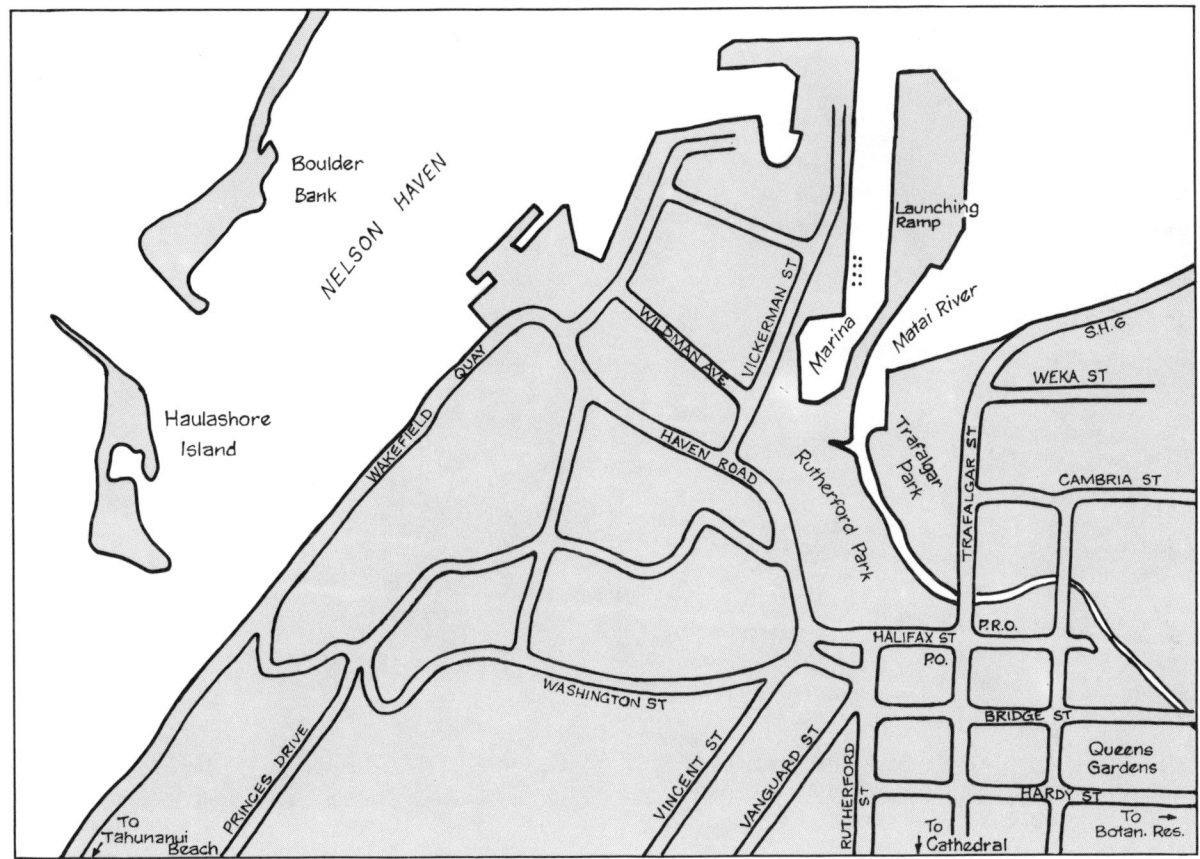

You will probably visit Nelson on your way to Abel Tasman National Park as it is the main provisioning point for deep-draught boats and provides a pleasant break if you are travelling with a boat on a trailer.

It has a variety of accommodation for visitors, from plush hotels to camping grounds and a youth hostel. Full details can be obtained from the information centre on the corner of Halifax and Trafalgar Streets in the main shopping centre.

Nelson is a major port used by fishing boats and ships carrying such things as wood products for export. The activity in the harbour will be of interest to children travelling with you. The harbour is being developed and facilities for small craft expanded. This area is called the Maitai reclamation and is to the left of the big ship port as you enter from seaward.

Anchorage

Nelson is a tidal harbour but it is possible to enter at any stage of the tide. There is a large boulder bank running for many kilometres to the east of the harbour but this is quite obvious and the entrance is between the end of the boulder bank and Haulashore Island. The channel is well marked. Keep to the channel to avoid the sandbank to port entering. Small boats should head right down the harbour past the big boats to starboard. Turn into the Dixon Basin by the fishing boat wharf, go down to the end and tie up to the floating dock on the starboard side, just before the entrance to the pleasure boat harbour.

Visitors' berths are arranged by the small-craft supervisor, at the Nelson Harbour Board office at the far end of Wildman Avenue – the wide road

Nelson Harbour

with a grass median strip, across the road from the garage. If you want to live aboard your yacht while visiting Nelson there are pile moorings available. However, if you have accommodation ashore a temporary mooring will be arranged in the pleasure boat harbour.

Nelson Harbour Board is very kind to visiting boaties — the first week is free, then it is $1.32 per metre per week with a maximum stay of 28 days — that is, three more weeks after the first free week. Longer stays are at the harbour-master's discretion.

Launching ramp

There is a concrete ramp in the Maitai reclamation area with ample parking.

Recreation

Nelson is full of interesting old buildings, parks and gardens and craft shops which provide interest in a walk around the city. Pamphlets on city walks are available from the Public Relations Office, but it is fun just to wander. Walking from the harbour towards town you will come to Anzac Park in Halifax Street. Across the other side of the main street between Bridge Street and Hardy Street East are Queens Gardens — take your stale bread for the ducks.

Walk up Botanical Hill to the 'Centre of New Zealand'. It takes about 20 minutes each way starting from the Botanical Reserve in Milton Street. From the top there are good views over the city and port. Beside it is Branford Park at the start of the Maitai Valley. Take the Maitai Valley road off Nile Street and you will come to a park with fireplaces, swimming holes and picnic spots. There is a children's playground with flying foxes.

Cathedral
Nelson Cathedral set on Church Hill at the end of Trafalgar Street is the third building on the site.

Construction started in the 1920s: it is built mainly of Takaka marble. Queen Victoria proclaimed Nelson a Cathedral City in 1857 when the second wooden building was the parish church.

Entrance to the cathedral is up the steps and through the gardens to the main entrance at the far end of the building. Guides are available to conduct visitors around the cathedral during the holiday season. Services are held at 8 a.m., 10 a.m. and 7 p.m. on Sundays.

Suter Art Gallery

Adjoining Queens Gardens, this gallery contains one of the best art collections in New Zealand. The original building was built in 1898 to house the collection bequeathed by Bishop Suter; it was extensively modernised in 1979. The complex also includes a restaurant and craft shop and is open daily.

Founders Park

Along the coast going east from the city centre in Atawhai Drive is Founders Park, which shows aspects of Nelson past, present and future. Leisure activities are combined with exhibits. It is a working museum of industry, transport, commerce and trades and is open daily from 10 a.m. to 4.30 p.m. Devonshire teas and lunches are available.

Tahunanui Beach

Westwards from the city five kilometres along the coast is Tahunanui, which features many leisure activities and a lovely sandy beach. Attractions include Natureland, a combined zoo and aviary, a modellers' complex, featuring a large pond for model boats and a miniature railway, hydro-slide, bumper boats, miniature golf, roller-skating, tennis courts and children's playground. There is also a motor camp. Buses serve the area but it is a pleasant walk along the coast for the energetic.

Nelson Yacht Club

The clubhouse is opposite the harbour entrance at 322 Wakefield Quay, Port Nelson. Postal address: PO Box 5058, Nelson. It is open weekends and 5 to 8 p.m. Friday. The club hosts the finish of the annual cruising races from Wellington and Ship Cove and the biennial Devonport to Nelson race.

Nelson Indoor Sports Centre

Tenpin bowling and other indoor sports are found at the centre, 34 Vanguard Street.

Abel Tasman National Park

Chart No: 614 Tasman Bay
Chart No: 6143 Totaranui and
Awaroa Anchorages
Map No: Infomap Parkmap 273-7

Facilities

The main provisioning centres for people approaching the park by road are Motueka on the southern approach and Takaka on the road to the northern entrance. Marahau has a little canteen for ice-creams and soft drinks and there is a shop at the Kaiteriteri motor camp. There are no shops in the park. Deep-draughted boats will have to provision in Nelson.

 FUEL   Takaka, Pohara camp, Kaiteriteri, Motueka, Nelson.

 GAS   Takaka, Motueka, Nelson.

 WATER   Totaranui camp, Torrent Bay, Adele Island, Marahau. There is a water buoy at Bark Bay for boats and it is safe to use the fresh water in the streams in the park.

 STORES   Takaka and Motueka are townships with all the usual services such as grocery store, butcher, chemist, post office, bank and garages. Nelson has a full range of services.

 RUBBISH DISPOSAL   visitors to the park are asked to take away their own rubbish and dispose of it outside the park. However, if this is not possible there are collection points at Awaroa, Bark Bay, Anchorage and Totaranui.

 TOILETS   Totaranui, Kaiteriteri, most camping areas along the coast.

 SHOWERS   Torrent Bay.

 RANGER   Chief Ranger, 1 Commercial Street, Takaka; telephone Takaka 58-026. Office hours 9 a.m. to 5 p.m. Monday to Friday. High Street, Motueka; telephone Motueka 89-117; 9 a.m. to 5 p.m. Monday to Friday. There are also rangers in the park during the summer.

 TELEPHONE   the park huts have emergency radios and there is a telephone at Totaranui and Torrent Bay.

 POLICE   Takaka 59-211.

 FIRST AID   doctors' surgeries in Takaka and Motueka.

 LOCAL RADIO   Radio 2ZN 1341; marine conditions broadcast hourly after news.

 WEATHER FORECAST   from Nelson Meteorological Office; telephone Nelson 729-920.

 DIVE AIR   at Junction Hotel, Takaka, and Sports and Dive Centre, Motueka.

 TRANSPORT   A bus service runs from Nelson via Motueka to both ends of the park. A boat operates from Kaiteriteri dropping off and collecting people at several points along the coast. It is necessary to book the boat, particularly if you want picking up, so the skipper knows to look out for you.

 ACCOMMODATION *Camp grounds* at Pohara (10 km from Takaka), Totaranui, Marahau, Kaiteriteri, Motueka.

 Huts at Anchorage, Torrent Bay, Bark Bay, Awaroa, Whariwharangi Bay on the coast and on the inland track at Awapoto, Wainui, Moa Park and Castle Rock.
Hotels/motels on the roads to the park such as Takaka and Motueka. However, the beauty of the Abel Tasman National Park is that you can make your own camp in a suitable spot, provided you abide by the park rules.

Abel Tasman National Park is situated on the north coast of the South Island. It covers almost 22 000 hectares and extends from Separation Point in the north to Marahau in the south.

Its main attractions are the sandy beaches, walks, and boating activities. There are great contrasts of scenery from the rolling high country, scrub-covered bluffs and deep gorges to the gently curved golden beaches formed by the breaking down of the granite cliffs. In many bays the bush grows down to the high tide mark.

Sea-birds such as shags, gannets, terns and blue penguins abound and the estuaries attract oyster-catchers, stilts and herons. Seals and dolphins may be seen offshore.

Much of the park is forest with one or more beech species dominant. On more fertile sites jungle-like warm-temperate rain forest is found, with vines, perching plants and tree-ferns. The early pioneers cleared much of the forest but it is now regenerating.

Anchorages

There are no suitable anchorages from Totaranui north around Separation Point until Tata Islands. A dangerous sea can build up around Separation Point and it is best to go round when wind and tide are in the same direction. The first bay suitable for boaties is Totaranui but it is very exposed to both easterlies and westerlies.

Launching ramps

Totaranui – Concrete, usable three hours either side of high tide. Busy in summer.

Kaiteriteri – Concrete, usable except one and a half hours either side of low water springs (high tide 17 minutes before Nelson). It is very congested in summer and trailers cannot be parked near the ramp.
Motueka – Two hours either side of high tide (high tide 12 minutes before Nelson). Busy in summer. Cars and trailers can also be left at Marahau, but no all-tide ramp.

Recreation

Walking maps and further information on the park are available from the information centre in Nelson on the corner of Halifax and Trafalgar Streets, the Department of Conservation, Nelson, Motueka and Takaka and the visitor information centre at Totaranui (open mid-December to mid-February).

Each year thousands of trampers from all parts of the world walk through Abel Tasman National Park. A boat service drops trampers at points along the coast to pick up tracks; a bus service travels to Totaranui or Marahau.

There are no jetties in the park. Trampers are transferred from the ferry to the beach by inflatable dinghy. Huts and campsites provide accommodation in the park. Three days is the recommended time for the full walk, starting at either end.

Tracks and huts
For boaties who wish to combine a boating holiday with a walk along the whole track here are the details of the times and huts. Perhaps you could leave your trailer boat at Totaranui and catch the ferry back at the end.

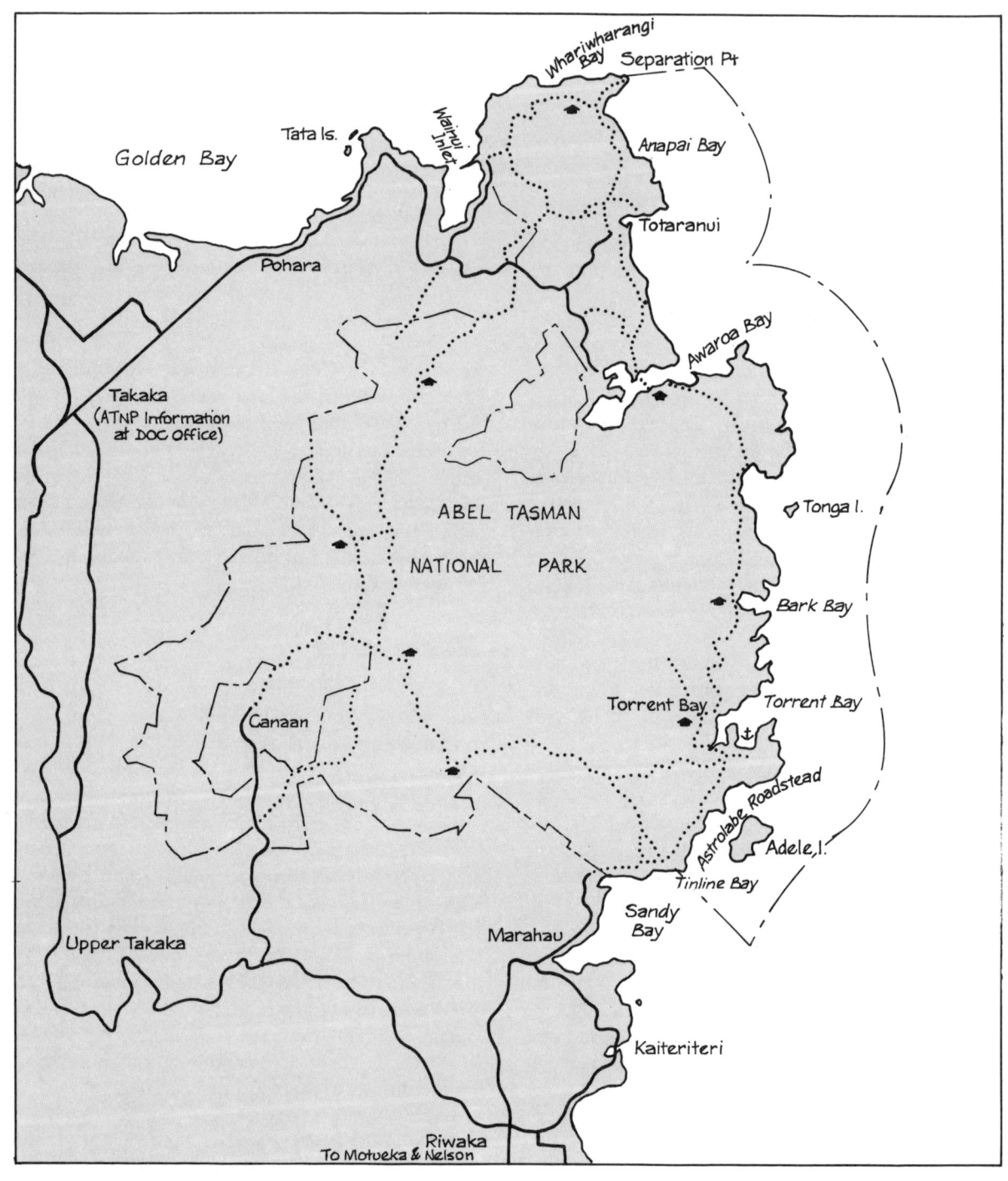

● Wainui to Whariwharangi Hut (26 bunks) – one and a half hours

● Whariwharangi Hut to Totaranui – three to four hours

- Totaranui to Awaroa Hut (26 bunks) – one and a half hours
- Awaroa to Bark Bay Hut (28 bunks) – three hours
- Bark Bay to Torrent Bay (8 bunks) or Anchorage (26 bunks) – three hours
- Torrent Bay to Marahau (the boat calls at Tinline Bay) – three to four hours

There are four estuaries along the coast which can cause delays if tides are not allowed for. Awaroa and Wainui Bay inlets can be crossed on foot only two hours either side of low tide. Torrent and Bark Bay have high tide tracks so can be negotiated if necessary. Tide-tables are placed in the huts and at either end of the walking track. Venture Creek and Tonga Swamp outlets can also cause delays at high tide.

at the start of each trip. If you are unsure about track information check with park staff.

Huts are provided with wood stoves, mattresses and bunks and water. Carry your own cooking stove and in summer take a tent in case the huts are full. The hut fee should be paid to the park staff or the Department of Conservation office.

Boating

Boating along the coast of Abel Tasman National Park is best suited to trailer sailers and runabouts which can get into the sheltered bays and lagoons or run up onto the sand and dry out. Beware of spring tides when drying out. The tide that carries your boat ashore may not be as high the next time. Activities suitable for the lagoons include dinghy sailing, canoeing, fishing and eeling.

Although most people have to take their holidays in the summer, the park provides good boating at other times of the year and the facilities are open all the year round.

There is only one decent deep-water anchorage for yachts. This is at Anchorage, Torrent Bay, which is very popular in summer. It is about three hours to Torrent Bay from Nelson at an average cruising speed. Adele Island has an anchorage on the west side but it is in the Astrolabe roadstead and not really protected from the sea. In an easterly wind there

is no shelter at all and easterlies often spring up without warning, creating short steep seas.

Divers will occasionally find crayfish and scallops in season. Diving is better in winter because the summer breezes disturb the water. Canoeing is also better in winter when the water is calmer. The seas are quite choppy in summer.

Fires

Fire is a major worry in the park because of the low, inflammable vegetation. Before lighting a fire, check with the ranger if there is a fire ban in force. Gas and liquid fuels are exempt from the fire ban, but barbecues are not allowed during fire bans.

If there is no fireplace provided, light fires below high water mark, not at the top of the beach underneath overhanging vegetation and never against logs. Make small fires and put them out when finished. Do not light fires if a strong easterly is blowing as it will spread inland through the gorse.

Unfortunately sandflies and mosquitoes like the park too so take plenty of insect repellant to keep them at bay. Bees and wasps are common in the summer, so people allergic to stings should carry the appropriate remedy.

Totaranui

Totaranui is a popular holiday spot with a big camping ground, visitor centre and long sandy beach. It is one hour's drive from Takaka over a winding metal road – we visited by bus and on one particular corner the driver had to ease the bus round while watching the sheer drop at the edge of the road through the open door! So people trailing boats and caravans take extreme care.

A large grassed area on the foreshore provides space for tents and caravans, and fresh water and toilets are provided. No power. There is a limit to the number of people the camp can hold so booking is essential if you intend to camp between 20 December and 31 January. Apply to the Department of Conservation, PO Box 53, Takaka.

There are no hut facilities so trampers stopping overnight at Totaranui will have to camp.

Domestic animals are not allowed in the park.

The beach is long and open. There are no trees to provide shelter from the sun. The low scrub reaches to the edge of the beach. It is a good beach for children to play on and they will also enjoy the estuary. Because of the open nature of the coastline at this point there is no sheltered anchorage for large boats. However, for runabouts and trailer sailers there is a launching ramp. There is also a ski lane for water-skiing enthusiasts.

The main walk running north to south through the park begins at Wainui, and Totaranui is a stopping point along the route. If you are spending a few days there you can do part of the walk and return.

There are also some short walks:
• Full day walk north to Separation Point with fine views, interesting rock formations and a wide variety of vegetation
• Pukatea Walk – 30 minutes from Totaranui return. Booklet available
• Anapai Beach – 40 minutes from Totaranui
• Te Mata O Te Moana – two hours from Totaranui return. Booklet available.

During the summer there is an organised holiday programme and the visitor centre is staffed from mid-December to mid-February.

Awaroa Bay

Awaroa is a major historical area and there are several short walks. The main walk passes through Awaroa's large estuary. If you are walking the track check the tide times – tide-tables are provided in the huts. It is good for seafood such as mussels, oysters, cockles, and scallops in season.

At half tide and below, the entrance to Awaroa should be navigated carefully. Watch particularly if a north-east or east wind is blowing as it creates surf on the bar. As with all the estuaries there is a strong tidal flow. Boats will find shelter in the eastern corner in south or east winds. Keep well offshore when moving down the coast to Tonga Island.

Tonga Island

This is not a safe anchorage and is not recommended unless the weather is really calm. Be prepared to move if the wind gets up. The northern end gives some shelter but dries.

Two points of interest are the seal colony on Tonga Island and the granite quarry which provided the stone used to build the Nelson Cathedral steps.

Bark Bay

Care must be taken entering Bark Bay because of the reef which stands nearly two metres clear at low tide. It extends from the south head for about 50 m northwards. If coming from the north beware of the series of rocks and sunken reefs sticking out from Mosquito Bay. Find Harleys Rock and turn in.

Bark Bay is an estuary so best suited to shallow-draught boats. It has a park hut, two camping areas – one on the sandspit and one inland – a safe beach which is steepish at high water but shallow at low tide, rubbish facility and a water buoy. The water buoy is hard against the north shore about half-way along.

Torrent Bay

The Anchorage in Torrent Bay is the most popular place on the coast for deep-draught boats. There are a few rocks in the bay and we were advised by an experienced local boatman to watch for the park track on shore and approach the bay with the track on our left (port-hand) – that is, to the right of the track.

A sea-breeze comes up each day, with December

Rocky coastline, Abel Tasman National Park

Kaiteriteri Beach

the worst time of the year when the winds are all over the place.

Facilities at Anchorage include a park hut, camping ground, fresh water, shower, rubbish disposal, open fireplaces, and an emergency radio in the hut.

The beach is sandy with no rips and is safe in all conditions except a pounding easterly. There is no shade on the beach so take your sun hats and cream. The lagoon provides a good place for sailing dinghies and canoes.

Torrent Bay is on the main coast walk through the park. There are also numerous short walks for visitors to the Bay suitable for all ages. For example:

- Pitt Head – one hour from Anchorage Hut return. Booklet available.
- Cascade Falls – one hour from Torrent Bay village.
- Cleopatra's Pool – 45 minutes from either hut at Torrent Bay.
- Torrent Bay Hut to the anchorage – 20 minutes at low tide or one hour along the track.

- Half-day walk to Pitt Head/Te Pukatea Bay followed by a visit to Cleopatra's Pool.
- Full-day walk north to the Falls River and Bark Bay lookout and return.
- Full-day walk in the Cascade Falls/Falls River area followed by a walk around Torrent Bay Lagoon and the Anchorage.

As with the other lagoon-type bays, Torrent Bay is particularly suited to trailer sailers and runabouts. These boats are usually short on accommodation space – especially if there are young children on board – so it is good to be able to put some of the crew ashore to camp and enjoy the open space.

As you enter Torrent Bay the lagoon is on the right-hand side. There are a few holiday cottages on the shore. It is only accessible at one and a half hours each side of high tide and the tide runs swiftly so beware. The lagoon covers several acres and there is room for about 20 boats. Some boats put out an anchor and a line to the shore. There are toilets and water ashore.

While based at Torrent Bay, small boats can make

day trips to Frenchmans Bay and Sandfly Bay up the coast. There are no houses or camp at Frenchmans Bay so it is a good place to get away from it all, but be careful of rocks as you enter. No camping allowed as it is private land.

Sandfly Bay is the entrance to the Falls River which is navigable by small boats two hours either side of high tide. Watch out for overhanging trees which could break a mast.

There is a privately owned tourist lodge in Torrent Bay. The owners offer a package holiday with transport to the lodge, guided walks, accommodation and meals all included. This is an ideal way to enjoy the park for those who do not have their own boat, trampers who do not want to carry all their own supplies and those who want a little more comfort than camping or park huts can provide. Details from John Wilson, Abel Tasman National Park Enterprises, Green Tree Road, RD3, Motueka.

Adele Island

The area between Torrent Bay lighthouse and Adele Island is known locally as the Mad Mile because of the many hazards in the area — mostly strong winds. Other hazards around the island are Hapuka Reef and Six Foot Rock to the north, and a sandspit off the south-west corner.

Because of the direction of the prevailing winds, Adele Island is a good place to head for from Nelson. There is an anchorage on the west side, but keep towards the mainland until the anchorage is in sight to avoid the sandspit.

There is no beach at high tide. There are rough tracks on the island but they are not suitable for children or older people. However, there are some caves for the children to play in.

Tinline Bay

Tinline Bay is the first/last deep water bay where trampers can be dropped off or collected from the coast track.

Kaiteriteri

Kaiteriteri is not in the park, but it is a good place to launch a boat for a visit to the park as it has sealed road access. It has some room for anchoring but shallows out a considerable distance and can be uncomfortable as an overnight anchorage. There is a rock marked with a pipe on the beach which is uncovered at low tide so beware if landing on the beach.

Motueka

Motueka has all the shops and services of a town. However, access from the sea requires negotiating a bar. Depth on the bar at high water spring tides is approximately four metres and three metres at high water neap tides. The channel is well defined and runabouts can get to the wharf at any stage of the tide. Beware of the strong current, particularly ebb spring tides.

Appendix 1 – Fishing information

Most people enjoy fishing. It is very satisfying to sit down to a meal you have caught and know is really fresh. However, there are some rules to be observed under the Fisheries Act 1983 which many boaties may be unaware of.

Do you know how many crayfish you can take in one day? Do you know the limit for blue cod in the Marlborough Sounds? And when you are passing through a school of kahawai and they are throwing themselves at the lure, do you know when to stop hauling them aboard?

Shellfish

The following table outlines restrictions for taking, possessing or conveying shellfish species. Keep in mind the seasons, which are listed later.

Shellfish species	Maximum daily limit per person	Minimum length (mm)
Cockles	150	
Kina (sea eggs)	50	
Mussels	50	
Oysters (dredge)	50	50
Oysters (rock & Pacific)	250	
Paua (ordinary)	10	125
Paua (yellow foot)	10	80
Pipi	150	
Scallops	20	100
Tuatua	150	

Toheroa may not be taken, possessed or disturbed unless a season is declared open.

No person may take paua and mussels using scuba gear or be in possession of paua or mussels while in possession of scuba gear.

Rock oysters cannot be opened while they adhere to the object on which they grow.

Oysters (rock and Pacific) can be taken all year in the North Island except from the Hauraki Gulf, Whangaruru Harbour and the Bay of Islands (excluding Te Puna Inlet).

Dredge oysters may only be taken from 1 March to 31 August.

Scallops may only be taken from 15 July to 14 February inclusive.

Shellfish recipes

Overseas visitors are sometimes unsure how to prepare shellfish they find along the New Zealand shore. The smaller types, such as pipis, cockles and tuatuas, can be used just like clams in chowders, soups and pasta dishes.

Here are two recipes kindly supplied by North American sailors Lin and Larry Pardey. Lin is famous for her clam chowder wherever cruising boats get together. For the New Zealand context pipis replace clams.

Pipi chowder
To prepare shellfish collected from the beach first soak in fresh water to expel sand. Cook in a little boiling water and remove meat as soon as shells open.

3 potatoes
1 onion
3 tbsp butter
prepared pipis
½ can evaporated milk
1 tsp MSG
1 tsp crushed garlic
salt to taste

Cut potatoes into small chunks and boil in salted water until cooked. Chop onion and sauté in butter. Add the rest of the ingredients to the potatoes. Heat until milk starts to simmer. Add salt if necessary.

Larry's pipi linguini

6 garlic cloves
3 tbsp olive oil
1/8 - 1/4 cup fresh chopped parsley (or 1/8 cup dried)
1 tbsp oregano
1/2 cup dry white wine
1/8 cup lemon juice
1/2 cup or more pipi meat
3/4 cup pipi juice
250 g linguini or egg noodles
1/4 cup parmesan cheese

Sauté garlic in olive oil, then add all but last two ingredients. Boil then drain pasta, add to above ingredients and toss well. Finally add parmesan, toss and serve immediately with a fresh green salad.

Rock lobsters (crayfish)

No person may take or possess more than six rock lobsters in one day. Spiny rock lobsters must not have a tail shorter than 152 mm and packhorse rock lobster tails less than 216 mm. They must not be carrying external eggs or be in the soft shell stage. No person may take rock lobsters which cannot be measured, and it is an offence to remove external eggs or the egg-bearing appendages from rock lobsters.

Lobster tails are measured from the posterior side of the calcified bar on the under-side of the first segment to the tip of the telson of the tail fan measured in a middle straight line.

Fishing gear: It is an offence to use any device which could puncture the exoskeleton when taking rock lobsters, to set a rock lobster pot unless it is marked by a surface float carrying the fisherman's surname and initials, and set or possess a rock lobster pot unless it has an escape gap measuring at least 54 mm in height and 300 mm in width.

Fin fish

The following table gives restrictions for taking, possessing and conveying fin fish species.

Fish species	Minimum net mesh size (mm)	Minimum fish length (cm)	Maximum daily limit per person
Blue cod		30	30*
Blue moki	115	40	30
Butter-fish	108	35	30
Eels	12		none
Elephant fish	150		30
Flat-fish (except sand flounder)	100	25	30
Garfish (piper)	25		none
Groper			30
Herrings	25		none
Kahawai	85		30
Mullet	85		none
Pilchard	25		none
Red cod	100	25	none
Red moki	115	40	30
Rig	150		30
Sand flounder	100	23	30
Snapper	100	25	30
Terakihi	100	25	30
Trevally	100	25	30
All others	100		none

*Except in the Marlborough Sounds, Golden Bay and Tasman Bay area where 12 is the daily limit.

Netting – no person may set, use or possess more than one drag net, set net or fyke net or any other type of net at any one time.
– nets must be hauled by hand.
– no net or nets used either individually or jointly may be extended more than one-third of the way across the width of any river, stream or channel.
– no person may set or use a baited net.

Set nets:
• must not exceed 60 m in length.
• must not be set within 60 m of another net.
• must not be used with stakes.
• must have a surface float marked with the fisherman's surname and initials on each end.
• must not be set or used to strand fish.

Drag nets:
- must not exceed 40 m in length.
- must not have a warp that exceeds 200 m in length.

Line fishing   – all surface floats attached to any line must be marked with the fisherman's surname and initials.
     – no person may use more than one line (other than handlines or rod and reel lines) or use or possess a line having more than 50 hooks.

This may look like more bureaucratic red tape to spoil our fun, but it protects the fish so that there will always be plenty more fish in the sea for everyone.

Appendix 2 – Diving information

The following information on diving was prepared with the help of Kevin Butler who is well known in Northland for his diving information programme. He broadcasts on Radio Northland at 8.15 a.m. on Saturday and Sunday during winter and every day during summer.

Kevin is a PADI (Professional Association of Diving Instructors) master instructor and charter boat skipper. He has been a diving instructor for nearly 30 years and he and his wife run a charter boat operation and dive shop in Whangarei.

Poor Knights Islands

One of the best diving areas in New Zealand is around the Poor Knights Islands, which lie 15 miles off the Northland coast. The water is very clear and there are dives for all levels of experience.

The area is a marine reserve, part of the Hauraki Gulf Maritime Park. There are many subtropical fish and other creatures seen nowhere else around New Zealand. The group comprises two large islands, Aorangi and Tawhiti Rahi, and numerous smaller inlets, stacks and rocks, covering an area of 267 hectares and rising to a height of 240 m above sea level.

Most of the islands are bounded by sheer cliffs, some plunging to 90 m below sea-level. There are 16 large caves above and below water and 14 rock archways through which quite large boats can pass.

Because it is a marine reserve no fish can be taken and no landing is allowed on the islands. There are places to anchor while diving but no overnight anchorages. The closest anchorage on the mainland is Tutukaka 14 miles to the west. Mooring buoys are provided in South Harbour, Aorangi Island.

The water around the Poor Knights is very clear and distances can be deceptive. It is most important to monitor gauges because people sometimes get into trouble by heading for something that looks close, only to find they have gone further than they should. Decide your maximum depth before diving and keep to it.

Nursery Cove

Nursery Cove at the top of Aorangi Island is the most popular diving area at the Poor Knights. The depth is from 3 to 15 m. Even non-divers can put their faces in the water, watch the fish and listen to the bellbirds and tuis on the land. The fish will take bread out of your hand.

Anchoring in Nursery Cove requires a grapnel because it is rocky but further out there is white sand with 15 to 20 m depth of water.

Just below Nursery Cove on the west coast of Aorangi Island is the Garden Patch off El Torito Cave. Diving is in 10 to 20 m among weed with no current.

Other dives suitable for novices are Blue Maomao Arch on Archway Island and South Harbour, Aorangi. Among the myriad of colourful fish to be seen are sand daggers, blue maomao, demoiselle, butterfly perch and trevally.

The Tie Dye Arch on the Pinnacles is another safe dive, except when there is an easterly swell. And it is pretty – exactly as the name implies. Navigators should beware of the rock just below the surface to the south of the Pinnacles. It drops away sharply and at low tide there is broken water around the rock.

Caves

For the more experienced diver there is an underwater air bubble cave – Bernies Cave – midway along the west coast of Tawhiti Rahi Island. Although the cave is 15 m long only 10 m shows on the depth gauge. To find the bubble, anchor in the bay then look for the arch. Bernies Cave is just to the left, on the south side of the arch.

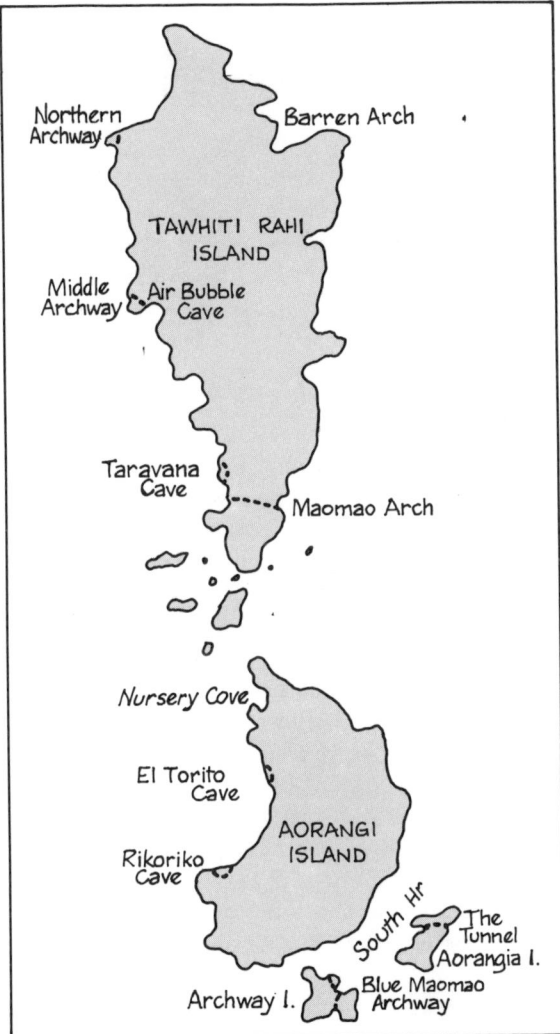

Tunnel, Aorangi Island. Northern Arch is a spectacular dive but it is too narrow for boats and at times there is quite a surge.

Hen and Chicken Islands

This group of one large and several small islands was named by Captain Cook. The group is included in the Hauraki Gulf Maritime Park and lies just off the entrance to Whangarei Harbour (9 miles from Busby Head). Though the diving is good, it is affected by the strong current which buffets the islands.

As with the Poor Knights, no landing is permitted on the islands, but the Hen and Chickens are a nature reserve, not a marine reserve, so fish and crayfish can be taken.

The main island, the Hen, is Taranga Island. Lady Alice, Whatupuke and Coppermine are the largest of the 11 chicks and there are good overnight anchorages in South Cove, Lady Alice Island, and Boulder Bay and Starfish Bay, Whatupuke Island. Do not pass between Whatupuke and Coppermine.

The best fishing is off the north coast of Coppermine Island. Diving is most spectacular around Tara Rocks but is affected by the current. If the flow is north to south there will be kingfish, snapper and trevally, but not if the flow is east to west. There is a one-hour difference between the tides here and at Whangarei Harbour.

Whangarei Harbour

Urquharts Bay, McLeods Bay and Snake Bank in Whangarei Harbour are all good for scallops in season but watch the strong current.

Just outside the harbour good diving areas are Smugglers Bay and Peach Cove.

Northland coast

Diving is good all the way up the coast. There are three major gables and it gets better as you go further north. There are no big rips and many of the diving spots can be reached by driving to the beach and swimming out.

Taravana Cave on the west coast of Tawhiti Rahi Island is also for the experienced only. It goes to 20 m and contains a deadman's arm. Nearby is Maomao Arch which goes from 9 m to 12 m west to east.

Divers and non-divers can enjoy the thrill of taking a boat through archways and into caves. On the west coast of Aorangi Island is Rikoriko Cave, which has 28 m of water and 30 m clearance. Game-fishing boats can turn around in here and there are stories of submarines using it during the war.

Boats without masts or outriggers can pass through Southern Arch, Archway Island and The

The coast at the end of Kauri Mountain Road, Ocean Beach, is a good crayfishing area, and Taiharuru Harbour is known for snapper and kina, but all along the coast there are fish and shellfish to be found.

Deep-draught boats and yachts should beware of Elizabeth Reef just north of the entrance to Whananaki River.

Cape Brett

There are big tides and currents with much water movement around Cape Brett and it is not a place for novices. There are rips around Dog Island but spectacular fishing. Keep clear of the 'Hole in the Rock' on Piercy Island as charter boats regularly take their passengers through.

The Marlborough Sounds

The Marlborough Sounds have many wrecks to explore, including the Russian cruise ship *Mikhail Lermontov*, which sank in Port Gore in 1986. There is also a wealth of scallops, crayfish and reef fish for the underwater fisherman.

Just out of Picton, off Double Cove, is the coastal trader *Koi*. It is lying in 20 m of water and is almost intact. A local dive club has sunk an old launch off Karaka Point at the head of Waikawa.

In the Cape Jackson area there are two wrecks. The *Lastingham*, a passenger cargo steamer, sank in 1884 on the west side of the Cape just a short distance from its destination of Wellington after a long voyage from England. Bottles and crockery have been found around the wreck, which lies in

up to 40 m of water.

On the east coast of the Cape is the coastal steamer *Rangitoto*, which sank in 1873. It is lying in 12 m of water.

An easy dive is the *Gazelle*, a sailing barque, which lies in 10 m of water at Okuri Bay just south of D'Urville Island. It came to grief in 1894 just five years before the steamship *Koranui* went down near Sauvage Point on D'Urville Island. The *Koranui* is lying in 20 m.

The *Mikhail Lermontov* is probably the best known wreck in the Marlborough Sounds because it went down so recently. One Russian seaman was lost, but miraculously the rest of the crew and all 409 passengers, mainly Australians, were saved.

The wreck is lying in about 40 m of water at the deepest point, but interesting dives can be made to about 15 m. There is only a metre or two of visibility so a safety line is essential and all care must be taken. The ship is still in one piece but the gash in the bow which caused the sinking is easily visible and large enough to swim through.

For those more interested in what they can find to eat than look at, scallops, crayfish and reef fish are found in most parts of the Sounds. Even close to Picton there are scallops on the shore of the Grove Arm and on the northern coast of Queen Charlotte Sound. They are also found in Kenepuru Sound, along the shore around Bulwer and Port Ligar, Port Gore and the eastern shore of Pelorus Sound.

Reef fish such as moki and butter-fish are found through Tory Channel and the outer sounds and along the east coast to Port Underwood. Blue cod are also plentiful for the line fisherman. D'Urville Island has the biggest crayfish but they are found off many other headlands around the Sounds.

Appendix 3 — Further reading

Abel Tasman National Park Board. *A Park for All Seasons — The Story of Abel Tasman National Park*, ATNPB, 1985.

Bay of Islands Maritime and Historic Park Board. *The Story of the Bay of Islands Maritime and Historic Park*, BIMHPB, 1985.

Bradstock, Mike. *Between the Tides*, David Bateman, 1988.

British Admiralty. *New Zealand Pilot*, 14th edition, 1987.

Coutts, Craig. *Coastal Yacht Navigation*, Heinemann Reed, 1988.

Falla, R.A., Sibson, R.B., Turbott, E.G. *Collins Guide to the Birds of New Zealand*, Collins, 1985.

Francis, Malcolm. *Coastal Fishes of New Zealand — A Diver's Identification Guide*, Heinemann Reed, 1988.

Hamilton, M., Battersby, P., Whiting, D. (eds). *The Royal Akarana Yacht Club Coastal Cruising Handbook*, Royal Akarana Yacht Club, 1986.

Hauraki Gulf Maritime Park Board. *The Story of the Hauraki Gulf Maritime Park*, HGMPB, 1983.

Kerikeri Marine Radio Association. *Bay of Islands Grid*, KMRA, 1988.

Kinsky, F.C., Robertson, C.J.R. *Handbook of Common New Zealand Birds*, Heinemann Reed, 1988.

Pardey, Lin and Larry. *The Care and Feeding of the Offshore Crew*, W.W. Norton Co., 1980.

Watkins, Janet M. *Pickmere Atlas of Northland's East Coast*, New Zealand, Janet M. Watkins, 1987.

Salmon, J. *Field Guide to Native Trees of New Zealand*, Heinemann Reed, 1986.

Sivess, Geoff. *Boatmaster*, Heinemann Reed, 1984.

Von Kohorn, R., Murray, K. *Cursing Guide: Cape Palliser to Marlborough Sounds and Tasman Bay*, Steven William Publications, 1982.

Whiting, P. *Penny Whiting's Sailing Book*, Heinemann Reed, 1984.

Index of place names